The Complete
Field Sales Program

The Complete
Field Sales Program

Gerard J. Carney

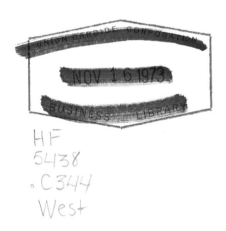

amacom

A Division of American Management Associations

International standard book number: 0–8144–5338–4
Library of Congress catalog card number: 73–80182

First printing

Contents

Introduction

THE phrase "a market-oriented company" is a heady one. It evokes a picture of dynamic executives, risking much for great rewards, not very well disciplined or controlled, making big mistakes but gaining greater victories, and triumphantly sweeping aside the penny-pinching, single-minded competitor. The company is dominated by the marketing department, which overshadows production, finance, and even research.

Wrong, all wrong. The truth is that no business is more single-minded, more penny-pinching than a market-oriented company. It concentrates all its resources on serving a specific buying group, and it wastes nothing. Its executives are dynamic, but in a superbly disciplined way. Gone are the operating straitjackets, the departmental barriers, the rigid thought processes of yesterday—all replaced by the toughest criterion of all: doing things the way the customer wants them done. Organizationally, there is no dominant department—not marketing, not finance, not production, not research. The buyer is the dominant force, and the market-oriented company says, "We are in business to serve a particular segment of the market, and value is in the eye of the beholder. The customer decides what is worthwhile, and he controls our actions. Everything we do must add value and help create sales, or else we must stop doing it."

1

Every business is a blend of constants and variables, and it is in the handling of the variables that market orientation stands out clearly. The constants are those activities that tend to follow regular patterns; the shipping department, the accounting procedures, and the personnel functions are examples of relatively fixed operations. Then there are the magnificent variables, the adventurous areas where the possibilities are endless, and the mind can soar. Research that produces a totally new process or raw material, or an advertising campaign that attains new levels in communication impact, both attest to the opportunity to stretch the limits of the company's ability, and then to stretch them again.

The field sales program is also one of the major variables, a blend of countless options. It can involve one salesman or many, can cover one metropolitan area or the whole world. It can serve the user directly or through many variations of multistep distribution. The sales force can be organized on a full-line or product or market basis. The challenge is to build a skilled team, of the correct size, properly equipped and motivated, to reach the company's sales goals — and there's the rub. For to define the sales goals means to define what markets the company serves and what objectives it wants to attain. Field selling is the external expression of the whole mission of the company and must be founded on a complete and realistic corporate plan.

The purpose of this book is to show how to develop a complete field sales program that is worthy of a market-oriented company. The final result must be imaginative, but based on facts and on tested selling principles. It must insure ample sales effort, but at a selling cost that the business can afford. Above all, it must be built step by step in a logical, disciplined sequence. This orderly process of examination and decision making falls into five distinct phases.

Phase 1: Creating a Market-Oriented Company
- Defining its business mission and its key strategies
- Developing a decision-making process based on facts and figures
- Building a complete profit plan, including a marketing plan

Phase 2: Planning and Organizing the Field Sales Effort
- Defining and measuring the sales task
- Formulating the customer and prospect coverage plan

- Setting the structure of the sales force
- Determining its size and location

Phase 3: Staffing, Training, and Motivating
- Recruiting the sales force
- Developing skills
- Motivating superior performance

Phase 4: Creating Selling Programs
- Designing the merchandising program
- Providing the selling tools

Phase 5: Leading, Appraising, and Improving
- Directing the field sales force
- Measuring and improving performance

A Few Definitions

A MARKET   A market is a common meeting place where title is transferred at a price one party is willing to pay and the other is willing to take.

A MARKET SEGMENT   Most human activity involves satisfying personal needs or contributing to the marketing process, either as a producer or a consumer. In such a vast arena, segmentation is bound to occur, and success comes to the marketer who defines the segment he serves, understands the forces operating, and then creates something to match the unique requirements of his buyer. Two components, supply and demand, must be identified if a market segment is to be accurately described. Supply refers to the goods or services offered; demand, to those who will buy and to the needs that are filled. For example, cleaning is a supply function, but there can be dry cleaning of clothing, steam cleaning of industrial engines, and sandblasting of dirty buildings. Buying for resale is a demand function, and includes buying an electric motor to sell as a replacement item (jobbing or distribution), buying it to incorporate in a machine that will be sold (original equipment manufacturer), and buying a used motor to sell its components for scrap.

MARKETING   Marketing is the development, acquisition, and sale of products or services in a manner and quantity that will attain the company's profit objective. Marketing starts at the very beginning, the first thought of organizing a business, and controls every function. Marketing is more than merchandising; it includes determining the customers' needs and acquiring the ability to fill those needs by manufacturing or buying products for resale, or by creating a service capability. The objective of marketing is to reach a specific profit target set for one company for one period. Because this concept includes profit responsibility, it applies to every department—whether the title be sales or production or finance. Everybody is a marketing man, and the company is market oriented because everything it does is critically evaluated in terms of the market segments it serves.

THE VALUE-ADDED PHILOSOPHY   The self-examination that is the heart of market orientation can be thought of as value-added philosophy, meaning "all value added has the objective of making a profitable sale." Literally interpreted, and it must be interpreted literally, it means that marketing expense is equal to the difference between the final selling price and the original raw material cost. Value added acts as a brake on unnecessary expenditures which cost more than the customer is willing to pay, such as a too-expensive raw material or package or too many steps (and costs) in the distribution chain. Conversely, it encourages adequate spending, because the customer will, sooner or later, reject the product that is below the performance or quality standard he wants. Finally, the value-added philosophy turns the spotlight on departmental expenses that increase cost without an equivalent increase in benefit to the customer. The manufacturing tolerances, the record-keeping system, even the executive suite are subject to the same test: "Is this necessary to serve our customer and will he pay for it?"

THE MARKET-ORIENTED COMPANY   A company is market oriented when it has analyzed its strengths and weaknesses, selected specific and logical market segments to serve, and concentrated every effort on providing the highest possible ratio of user benefit to user cost.

How to Use This Book

Each component in the development of a field sales program is analyzed in the following chapters. Examples and illustrations of sales management techniques are used extensively, and each chapter contains a checklist to aid in appraising the state of the company's current sales effort. Long discussions of individual aspects of field selling are omitted; many fine books concentrating on specific subjects are already on the shelf.

The purpose here is to say, "This is what should be in a complete field sales program. If you will agree or disagree with what follows, the end result will be what you believe should be in your individual program. At the same time, you can be deciding whether you will start at the very beginning and build or modify your entire program, or whether you will concentrate on one or two components that offer great opportunity for improvement."

Read the book from start to finish, preferably at one sitting (it will take less than three hours), to help clarify your ideas about the overall efficiency of the field effort. Look at the checklists, but don't take the time to fill them out. Your first goal should be to appraise the total situation. Ask others who have important roles in sales management to read this book. Specific ideas about action programs will begin to develop. Then, start through the book again, this time completing the checklists and confirming or changing your initial feelings about the key points that need attention. Whatever action is taken as a result of the evaluation will be based on an intelligent and candid appraisal of the sales program, and the priorities for effort will be realistic.

1 / Setting the Stage

THIS chapter briefly analyzes Phase 1 in the development of a complete field sales program — creating the market-oriented company. Its three steps are:

- Defining the company's business mission and its key strategies
- Developing a decision-making process based on facts and figures
- Building a complete profit plan, including a marketing plan

Phase 1, Step 1
Defining the Business Mission and Key Strategies

Traditionally a company is thought of as having three goals: to survive, to earn a profit, and to grow. However, even when these objectives are applied to one particular enterprise, their relative importance may vary. The rate and direction of growth are infinitely variable, and part of the company may expand while another part is being liquidated. What is needed therefore is a policy, approved by the stockholders and supported by all company executives, that answers these questions:

What is the company's mission, what is it trying to accomplish, and what major activities does it pursue? What does the company hope to become? How would it like to be described ten years from now?

The response to these deceptively simple questions cannot be a vague recitation of platitudes. Just as strongly, the reply must avoid too much detail, too specific a definition of standards, too many taboos or faddish goals. One logical approach is to agree first on those preliminary judgments that must precede the final statement, that is, to look at the present before planning the future and find out where the company is today. Many companies have gone through this creative and rewarding exercise, and the results of their effort are an ability to mass their strengths and to avoid wasteful diversion of effort.

Describing the present business. Few working tools fit the sales management job as well as the simple grid or matrix. Frequent use of it can not only present a situation graphically and clearly, but can also encourage logical thinking so often needed and yet not always available. In describing the company's present business, one or a few grids can do a better job than many pages of prose. Exhibit 1 shows the distribution of sales volume for a company principally in the metalworking field. Across the top are listed the major product groups, or supply segments. Down the left side are the major demand markets. The numbers show the percentage of the company's sales volume derived from the sale of one product group to one buying segment. Two-thirds of the total is concentrated in the four circled market segments, and it is readily apparent what businesses the company is in.

Other versions of the grid may be even more meaningful. Instead of sales volume, the profits produced by each segment can be shown. Graphic portrayal is also possible of the breakdown by geographic regions, by high- and low-margin sales, or by any combination that is meaningful to the business. Kept simple, the resulting grids are a clear statement of present position.

Establishing criteria for making changes. Having assessed its present position, the company must now establish reasonably permanent standards by which to judge the moves it can make. It is difficult enough to plan for the future when the ground rules are clear; when they are not, all sense of direction is lost and the future becomes unplanned. What characteristics make a business venture attractive for the company? What negative factors must be defined as a screen against unwanted enterprises? How does the company capitalize on its strengths and minimize its weaknesses? Those who control the business must spell out the criteria they use and see that they are circulated; then they must live by them.

Exhibit 2 shows how one company expressed its thoughts about future moves, the future also including a searching review of all its present activities. The entire organization becomes more effective when the key executives say, "In directing our present business and our future growth, this is how we think and how we judge. If you want to know what our decision will be, measure your proposal against these yardsticks."

Defining the business mission. When the company has accu-

Exhibit 1. Distribution of sales volume by major product lines and principal markets served (as a percentage of total sales).

Major Product Lines

Markets Served	Structural Building Components	Mining Equipment	Vehicle Components	Earth-moving Equipment	Metal Furniture and Appliances	Printing and Packaging	Other Products and Services	Total
Building industry	(25)				1			26
Mines		(16)		4				20
Motor vehicle manufacturers			(15)					15
Retail trade					(10)	1	3	14
Government agencies				6		1	2	9
Other markets	1			4		4	7	16
Total	26	16	15	14	11	6	12	100

rately described its present business and set the standards by which it will judge itself, it can begin to define its business mission. The first question is that of survival, not necessarily of the business, but of its present major components. Does it see any fields that are so unattractive as to dictate cutting off present operations?

Once the existing activities have been scrutinized, the future can be examined. What is the basic goal that controls the very nature of the enterprise? Should the name of the game be vertical integration, backward into raw materials and forward into distribution? Would the company be better off as an intermediate processor, and should it therefore concentrate on developing additional products, still buying raw materials and still making only the first sale in the distribution sequence? Are financial constraints so tight as to dictate the rate of growth, or is it more a question of finding profitable use for the funds eager investors are willing to subscribe?

Deciding key strategies. The purpose of devising a strategy is to encourage the initiative of the tactical commanders, but within defined limits. For a business it means answering these questions:

What markets are to be served geographically, by type of customer or end use, and in terms of the needs to be filled?

How will these markets be served as regards the products or services to be offered, the method of producing them, and the method of marketing them?

What is the financial strategy, including original capital and permanent ownership; funding the operation; and the policy on profits, dividends, and reinvestment?

Will the organization be a functional one—marketing, production, finance, and development—on a company-wide basis? Would it be more efficient if it were structured in terms of its geographic markets, or its product and services, or its customers' needs and patterns of use? Should there be a combination of these alternatives?

Communicating the business mission and key strategies. How and when to state "why we are here, what we propose to do, and how we shall go about it" is not easy. Some companies have issued policy statements, but all too often they end up as wordy, somewhat pompous pronouncements and gain little readership. One otherwise dynamic company used a 73-word sentence as an opener— surely the definitive blend of everything that everybody could think of to throw in. And yet, there must be a meeting of the minds; the top men must agree.

Exhibit 2. Criteria used to evaluate proposed actions.

In assessing opportunities the company asks the following questions or tests the proposal against these norms.

Discouraging Criteria

Intense competition. Is the industry so dominated, or so attractive to others, that great difficulty can be expected in developing a profitable share of the market?

Inability to price realistically. Could substitute materials, imports, or industry overcapacity seriously restrict pricing policies and limit profits?

Lack of economies of scale. Will the proposed venture have no advantage over smaller competitors, or is the economic-size plant likely to be too big for the realistic market potential?

Inventory vulnerability. Is the product range so wide, or are style, seasonal, and climatic factors so critical, that major inventory problems could result?

Not a phased risk. Must heavy expenditures for machinery, inventory, and market development precede the earning of revenue? Is there no way for growth to take place in steps?

Encouraging Criteria

Inherent advantage, such as
    a. *Control of raw materials.* Are the principal raw materials ones that we already produce efficiently?
    b. *Related to our skills and experience.* Can we honestly say that we know the business and are good at it?
    c. *Captive market.* Is it a closed-circle venture with assured markets and predictable profits?

Difficult for others to compete with us, because of
    a. *High capital cost and modernization requirements.* Is the venture capital intensive and does it need substantial reinvestment of funds?
    b. *High research and development need.* Is success tied to extensive and continuing basic and applied research?
    c. *Needs sophisticated marketing.* Does it require comprehensive and highly skilled marketing?

Attractive profit potential, because of
    a. *High growth rate.* Does it have a broadening market base? Is the proposed product at an early stage in its economic life cycle?

Exhibit 2. (Continued.)

---

    b. *High value-added component.* Does the product sell for well above its material cost, with opportunities for processing innovation and efficiency?

    c. *Good lateral and vertical expansion prospects.* Is it a logical building block for our present or proposed operations? Can it lead to further integration? Does it make better use of facilities we already have?

    d. *Above-average return on investment.* Do the results attained by others in similar ventures, and our own projections, show a return on investment above our target rate?

    e. *Ripe for our entry.* Is it a business where a new entrant could make a marketing or manufacturing breakthrough? Do we have a special advantage?

One way to get a concise definition of the company's central aspirations is to bring the key executives and senior managers together and say to them, "Let's write the annual report that we hope to issue in ten years' time." Now the emphasis is on results, not on intangible concepts. The goal is to produce a brief document, not the usual ten-year plan replete with masses of figures. It can be very illuminating to ask those who operate the company to look into the future and to agree on these few points for the annual report to be issued ten years from now:

- The president's message to stockholders
- Sales volume and profits, by markets (both supply and demand segments, as shown in Exhibit 1)
- Major changes in the last ten years
- Financial summary, including balance sheet and profit-and-loss statement

Phase 1, Step 2
Developing a Decision-making Process
Based on Facts and Figures

A company that has defined its mission and strategies can readily create an intelligent plan for knowing what is going on and deciding what action to take as a result of that knowledge. In truth, such a management information system was probably the first tool used, and the very decision to organize the company was based on facts and figures, rather than surmise and guesswork. Most of the problems in organizing a superior decision-making process spring from confused objectives, hazy channels of authority, and poor definition of decision-making criteria. As a result, those who should be only recording information often don the mantle of critics. The demand for data, data, and more data places an unreasonable burden on line and operating units. In its extreme form, the breakdown of the decision-making process fosters the development of informal parallel systems, designed to prove that the basic data have been incorrectly interpreted, that the company's management information system is really a misinformation system. Instead of an orderly flow of facts and figures that lead to logical decisions, management finds itself mediating a continuing struggle between staff and line.

Market-oriented decision making. The essential difference between the market-oriented company and one that is self-centered is in the kind of data it acquires and the decisions that flow from the figures. All well-run companies want to know what happened and why. If the primary judgment is based on financial results, it can examine its internal operation by using some version of the Du Pont chart shown in Exhibit 3.

The market-oriented company makes such calculations, but then goes farther and seeks to know what is going on outside the company and what the future will bring. The introverted approach is to say, "We had a good (bad) year because we did (did not) do these things. Next year will be better (worse) because we will do. . . ." It is an intramural view, as though the company generated its own profits. The dynamic view widens the data sources. Decisions are based on what happened inside the company, as well as on what took place outside, in the environment. The information system must keep up to date on such diverse items as market share, new processes and materials, future demand characteristics, and changes in distribution techniques.

Essential data. While the company will certainly tailor its information system to its unique needs, corporate managers usually need the following data to make sound decisions:

Operating results, including profit-and-loss statement, balance

Exhibit 3. Calculating the rate of return on total investment (before income tax).

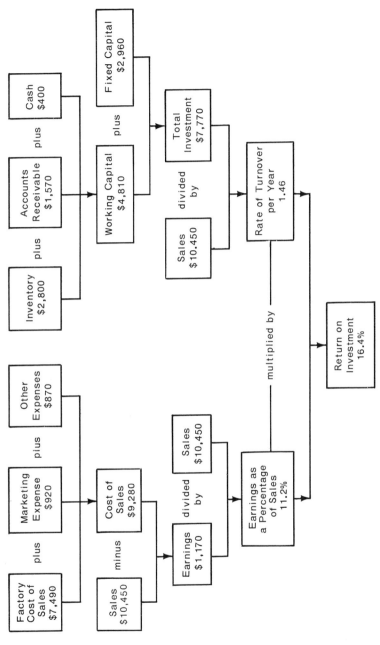

sheet, operating ratios, performance against plan, projection of future results, actual and projected cash flow.

Information about and analysis of departmental performance, including marketing, production, finance, administration, research and development, personnel.

Environmental analysis, including such factors as the marketplace, competitive activity, and social, political, economic, and technological factors.

Phase 1, Step 3
Building a Complete Profit Plan,
Including a Marketing Plan

A profit plan is an organized method of establishing periodic objectives and creating programs to attain them. It is more than a budget. In the strict sense, a budget is a projection of financial results. The profit plan includes a budget, but also spells out the actions the company intends to take to achieve its budget. Many alternatives are open within the broad strategies already defined. One company summarized the actions it could take under five broad headings:

Marketing
Increase product usage among present customers.
Increase product usage by winning new customers.
Serve new market segments.
Add new products.
Upgrade products and margins.
Expand services offered to customers.
Expand communications about products and company.
Reduce marketing costs.

Distribution
Widen geographic distribution area.
Change distribution methods.
Use additional distribution channels.
Reduce distribution costs.

Production
> Increase production capacity.
> Improve production efficiency.
> Speed inventory turnover.
> Perform more activities; integrate vertically.

Research and development
> Improve existing products.
> Develop new uses for existing products.
> Create new products.
> Develop lower-cost production methods or materials.

Organization and finance
> Restructure existing organization.
> Improve administrative efficiency.
> Merge with or acquire other companies or facilities.
> Dispose of unwanted facilities.
> Reduce working capital.

A profit plan consolidates the thinking of those who operate the company and those who own it, and promotes the unity of effort and decisiveness of action that a business must have. The three main benefits of a realistic profit plan are commitment, freedom, and concentration. *Commitment* comes first from the company executives, who say what they will accomplish; it is matched by the commitment of the shareholders, who, through the board, agree that the funds required to carry out the plan will be available. Next, a profit plan increases, rather than decreases, a manager's *freedom*, because it largely eliminates the need to ask for decisions. Within clear boundaries the manager is free to do as he wishes, provided he attains his promised objective. The third benefit, *concentration,* and often the key to winning any contest, means that all employees have their attention focused on the same set of objectives and concentrate their energies rather than scattering them.

Most profit plan problems arise when the original concept becomes distorted. A profit plan should be an individualized company exercise, and contain only the data needed for communication among people who are knowledgeable about the company. It should emphasize "nouns and numbers," not padding and approximations. When long background reports and statistical tables are required, the key men lose interest. They cannot spare the time required nor see the merit of the seemingly endless exercise. As a result, the work is assigned to those who have the time or who must find it. The profit plan no longer represents a joint and intense exercise by senior management. It is just another periodic report, earning neither commitment nor the creative spark.

The key elements of a company profit plan are listed in Exhibit 4. More important, however, is the thought process that evolves the plan. All the possibilities for action must be explored and the cost and benefit compared, always with a market orientation. What capital expenditures are proposed and how do they improve the ability to serve the company's customers? Have inventory levels been related to the market's needs or based on a production plan that looks only at history? Is the research and development program

Exhibit 4. Key elements of a company profit plan.

 I. The Chief Executive's Appraisal and Commitment
   1. Statement or restatement of company's mission and basic activities, its long-range goals, and its major strengths and weaknesses
   2. Appraisal of current year's expected accomplishments
   3. Appraisal of principal environmental factors
   4. Specific major objectives for the coming year
   5. Timetable of significant planned moves and changes
   6. Five-year forecast

 II. The Company Profit Plan
   1. Consolidated planned financial results and requirements
   2. Projections for interim periods (quarters or months)
   3. Summary of all departmental action programs, including concurrence by all department heads
   4. Correlation of proposed one-year plan with long-range goals and commitments

III. The Departmental Plans
   1. Appraisal of expected performance against current plan
   2. Appraisal of changes in internal or environmental factors
   3. Action programs for the coming year
   4. Planned profits and expenditures and financial requirements
   5. Long-range plans and their relation to coming year's programs

---

tied to marketing goals or is it considered uncouth to talk about sales and profits? When departmental plans are completed and coordinated, they are then summarized into one company program that represents the unified thought of those in authority. It is the expression of key executives planning key actions.

How often should a company plan? The annual profit plan is really a stop-action picture of a continuing process of creation, review, and change. Planning takes place every day, and progress should be continuous toward announced objectives. If there is one danger in formal profit planning, it is the temptation to separate those who plan from those who act. While the profit plan has its use as a periodic statement, it is not an end in itself. No one person should have the responsibility for planning unless he also has the responsibility for carrying the plan out. Individuals may be assigned the task of formulating a specific proposal, as for a brand introduction, or a move into a new market, or the re-equipping of a factory. Their work remains only a proposal until someone makes it his plan and also his operating responsibility. How often should a company plan? It can never stop planning. Action goes hand in hand with planning; the two cannot be separated, and the unplanned action is just as foolhardy as the plan that never gets action.

The Annual Marketing Plan

A vital component of Phase 1, Step 3 (the profit plan) is the annual marketing plan, and the field sales manager both contributes to it and is guided by it. Because the results his team produces are so visible and so measurable, he must pin down what he is expected to do and what help he can expect. Many years ago the famous labor leader Samuel Gompers, when asked to define the workers' goal, replied "More." The sales manager cannot receive such an inexact answer when he asks that his task be defined in terms of how much, where, and when. To allow him or to require him to make his own decision about these major objectives means both an abdication of senior executive responsibilities and a dispersion of resources. When each department manager begins to do his own thing, the market-oriented company degenerates into a loose confederation of autonomous and often conflicting groups.

A complete marketing plan should answer many questions (see Exhibit 5), and usually consists of 11 specific, measurable components.

1. Key marketing objectives and responsibilities
2. Market definition and appraisal
3. Products or services
4. Prices and terms of sale

Exhibit 5. Does your marketing plan answer these questions?

---

1. What marketing results are expected for the present year in comparison with planned objectives, programs, and budgets? If performance is not on plan, why? What lessons can be drawn?
2. What significant factors, both inside the company and in the marketplace, have changed since the last plan was made? What is the effect of these changes?
3. What share of the served market will be obtained in the coming year compared with this year's plan and expected performance?
4. What sales volume, composed of how many units, at what prices, will be attained during the coming year compared with this year?
5. What changes will be made in prices and terms of sale and in the policies and procedures that govern them?
6. What are the highlights of the program for communicating with customers and prospects, and for creating sales?
   a. What is the action program for the field sales force?
   b. What changes will be made in field selling programs, materials and methods?
   c. What is the program for merchandising, advertising, promotion, and public and customer information, and how is it coordinated with the field sales program?
7. What changes will be made in other marketing activities, such as physical distribution, technical service, and sales administration?
8. What is the planned cost of all these programs compared with this year, and stated in such ratios as percent of total sales or of gross profit?
9. What is the planned marketing profit (sales revenue less cost of goods sold, less marketing cost) for the coming year compared with this year?
10. What longer-range actions (more than one year) are planned, and how do they relate to the marketing plan for the coming year?

---

5. Merchandising program
6. Field sales coverage
7. Field selling program
8. Physical distribution
9. Support organization and programs
10. Direction, appraisal, and improvement
11. Planned revenue, expense and profit

The sequence of components may vary, as will their relative importance, depending on whether the business stresses promotion, logistics, price, technical service, or other purchase motivations. Until the marketing decisions are made, there is no agreement on who will do what and when. Can a business succeed without a formal marketing plan? Yes. Can a marketing plan be too voluminous, unattainable, and a waste of time? Yes. Can an intelligent middle course produce a plan that is tailored to the needs and capabilities of the individual enterprise? Absolutely. The following comments about the individual sections of the marketing plan may help the sales manager to visualize the framework within which he develops his own program.

1. Key objectives and responsibilities

The initial statements in the marketing plan should summarize the principal objectives and describe the team responsible for attaining them. This is not the place for reciting details already well known or for making premature arguments for justification of the various forecasts. It is, however, the place for a concise statement, which, added to equally succinct ones from other major departments, answers the question, "What are you going to accomplish next year?" The main points to be covered include:

Key financial data. Sales revenue forecast by dollars and units. Proposed marketing expense. Planned marketing profit (over defined cost).

Major subsidiary forecasts. By time periods, product groups, geographic regions, or specific programs.

Key marketing objectives. Narrative sentences pinpointing the important planned accomplishments, identifying significant changes, and providing a timetable.

Responsibilities. Listing only changes for the established marketing force or only highlights for the new organization.

As much as possible, this section should be an unqualified summary of what follows. It is the senior marketing executive's commitment, put together by his associates, but now his personal responsibility.

2. Market definition and appraisal

The company's basic decisions about marketing, production, and financial strategy have already clarified the broad geographic areas to be worked, the customers and prospects to be served, and the range of products or services to be offered. The marketing plan must be based on an appraisal of the entire potential of the served market, as designated by the company. Even if a deliberate decision is made that a given sector will not be covered, such a judgment can be made only on a 100 percent analysis.

More often than not, careful evaluation will show that the sales coverage can be expanded rather than contracted. It is generally easier to get 15 percent of a $100 million market than to get 30 percent of a $50 million one, although the resulting volume, $15 million, is the same. And yet a company will persist for years in ignoring the export market; in failing to find out all the products its customers buy; in deciding it won't make a real effort on the West Coast, or the East Coast, or through wholesalers, or to government agencies. The sad part is that the decision is not based on systematic appraisal; it just happens to be the way the business is run. What is needed in the market-oriented company is a three-step review that produces an intelligent analysis upon which all other marketing activities are based.

Definition of the served market. Within the strategic boundaries the company has set, sound marketing asks, "Who and where are all our potential customers, and what is the full list of products or services we could offer them?" Once this is known, even in broad terms, a deliberate cover or don't cover decision can be made for each major market segment. For example, one large group of mines issues annually a summary of all the goods and services bought, with the value of each category. Any company supplying even one product should analyze the list for market expansion possibilities.

When a product is sold to be used in a specific manufacturing process, then every company that uses the process is part of the served market and a potential customer. The goal in analyzing the full potential is to make sure that each market segment is worked as completely as possible.

Analysis of the market's characteristics. Having defined its market, the company must now understand the forces at work. Demand may be relatively constant or subject to wide swings. Competitive activity and environmental factors will affect the size of the market, but how much? The analysis now being made is an essential tool in deciding the product line, the entire marketing communication program, and the company's long-range plans. Major considerations include market size, location, and rate of change; buying motives, preferences, and objections; product or service mix now filling the demand; and new product developments and casualties among existing ones.

Short-term forecast. The potential of the served market and the many forces at work in it make one component of the short-term sales forecast. The other, of course, is the company's present sales results and the new or improved products it will offer. The result is a projection of the total market and of the share the company will obtain. The accuracy of the prediction depends largely on the data available. Automobile sales forecasts can be aided by exact records of past sales for all makes, but must then assess many hard-to-measure demand variables. New products may be so new that the best estimate that can be made is a projection of the rate of growth. The field sales manager has not only the right but the obligation to participate in this assessment of the future. Many companies include as a major forecasting tool a bottom up estimate made by the field group, starting at the territory level. It cannot be the only input, since the field sales force may not understand all the market forces at work or know all the future plans of other company departments.

One company made a concise definition and appraisal of a market segment with three grids:

Demand-supply. The annual market demand was estimated by forecasting the probable sales of each principal manufacturer in the major geographic markets.

Product-market share. The six principal product groups were divided according to the estimated sales of each leading manufacturer.

Product-customer type. The same principal products were analyzed by estimating who, as a type of customer, was buying them.

The resulting analysis, while not perfect, not only projected sales results for the next year, but also provided valuable guidelines for those looking at the product line, at proposed capital expenditures, and at the extent of the field sales coverage effort. By examining the served market from several viewpoints, the study encouraged first of all deep thought but after that, agreement on the marketing thrust.

3. Products or services

Once the market has been defined and measured it becomes possible to make sound judgments about the specific products or services to be offered. The sales force is not only interested in the range of products, but is often the chief influencing factor in decisions about what will be added, taken away, or changed. The value of the periodic marketing plan is that it insures coordinated activity and uniform priorities. Every day of the year new products are being developed, engineering changes are modifying existing products, and the market requirements which dictate product strategy are changing. Without the discipline of periodic review, those responsible can become overly interested in unimportant things, can get out of touch with the market, or simply not know what the other fellow is doing.

The products or services section of the marketing plan also provides advance signals about new markets that must be developed and understood by the field force. It indicates where effort can be curtailed, for example, if the company elects to go out of a certain business at some future date. Most important, however, is the guarantee that production, merchandising, and field sales all have the same instructions. A sound plan does away with unprofitable items that are easy to sell; with high-profit items that are high only in theory because no one will buy them; and with the other elephants and alligators that always seem to be cluttering up what ought to be a customer's buying list rather than a seller's offering list.

4. Prices and terms of sale

A market has been defined as a place where title is passed at a price one party is willing to take and the other party is willing to pay. What price will the company place on its products or services? Who decides the definition of cost, and what multiplier of cost must be used to attain desired profitability? How is the inevitable proposal to change a price reviewed and approved or disapproved? The field sales manager needs to know and the marketing plan should tell him. For his own sake, the manager should try to push the decision-making process down the organization as much as possible, so that he and his associates have clear authority within equally clear limits. He realizes that those who control the company may be fearful that giving him price latitude means that everything will be sold at the lowest price. He also knows that delays in handling pricing situations can mean lost sales, that he must be able to provide prompt answers to his buyer or prospect. The key requirement of this component of the marketing plan is clarity. The company is unique and its market conditions are unique; it must spell out three critical points:

Authority and responsibility for setting prices and terms of sale. The marketing department alone should not set prices and terms of sale, but neither should finance nor production. The annual plan provides a vehicle for assessing existing policies and proposing changes.

Financial guidelines. Markup over cost will produce adequate profits, provided the planned sales volume is attained and provided costs prove to be accurate. What financial rules must be followed in setting and administering prices?

Procedures for administration. If the price list contains discounts for certain classes of trade or for seasonal or quantity purchase, there will be many administrative decisions as to the exact price to be charged. Competitive activity can call for rapid price adjustments. A sound marketing plan defines the way to handle pricing situations swiftly and in accordance with company objectives.

5. Merchandising program
6. Field sales coverage
7. Field selling program

These three components of a marketing plan form a unit but their relative importance within that unit varies. Field sales effort can be of prime importance in reaching purchasing agents when technical products are involved, just as advertising in television and print is the principal medium to the housewife for grocery products. The total communication program is a blend of several components, each with a weight and relationship that fits the individual business.

The market-oriented company persists in its penny-pinching, single-minded attitude by insisting that the voice of the salesman, the written word, the visual message, even the field trips of key executives, be one unified effort. The objective is to get the customer to buy; and the message must be clear, it must speak of needs and values, and it must be complete. Each of the following chapters deals with the field sales components of the marketing plan and with how they fit into the total communication and merchandising program.

8. Physical distribution

The storage, transport, and delivery of his products are of such critical importance to the field sales manager that he is often given authority over these functions. Even if he cannot say what will be done, he needs to have a powerful voice in the planning phase and a clear channel for getting prompt decisions on distribution problems. It is not enough to have the production or distribution group make its own plan; marketing must concur, must agree that the arrangements are adequate and that the working relationships are clear. Traditionally, distribution is a prime area for vagueness of authority and responsibility, bruised feelings, and unhappy customers.

The principal concern should be the coordination of product inventory with sales patterns. It is going to one extreme to give the sales department sole authority to set stock levels or production schedules. The other extreme is to find warehouses cluttered with dead inventory shipped without notice from a factory that established its own manufacturing program. If agreement on inventory levels can be reached, the market-oriented philosophy (and not the marketing department) has triumphed, and the additional concerns of shipping procedures, record keeping, and customer service will be equally well resolved.

9. Support organization and programs

The marketing plan must provide for the smooth correlation of the selling effort with those support activities that provide service or furnish special assistance. The sales manager particularly wants clarification so that he can better define those duties he must perform beyond the conventional sales effort. He also wants to be sure that he knows where to turn for help and that the other party understands that help is to be given. Some of the categories of support organizations and programs include:

Marketing administration. In addition to recording marketing performance, administration can include invoicing, accounts receivable, inventory control, and other accounting functions that insure an orderly matching of the sale with the shipment and the collection of the proceeds.

Technical service. Varying greatly with the type of business will be activities designed to aid the technical aspects of a sale and to insure satisfactory performance after the sale. Programs can include engineering assistance, parts, service and repairs, warranty commitments, and periodic maintenance. The main concern is that each component of technical service see itself as a marketing tool, designed to insure the buyer's satisfaction and thereby increase the chances of repeat or new sales.

Personnel services. Certainly one of the major responsibilities of a sales manager is the team he develops. Within the company there may be help in recruiting, including appraisal of those who are already employed and who may be qualified for transfer to sales. Training, particularly in standard company procedures, and testing may be available. In the area of motivation the manager may be able to enlist expert help in developing both his compensation plan and the intangible rewards he must offer to win the best possible performance from his men.

Credit and collections. The collection of outstanding balances may be the complete responsibility of the sales force, or the credit and the sales functions could be separated completely. The marketing plan should define the relationship and indicate if it is satisfactory from a marketing standpoint. Needed changes, hopefully with the concurrence of the financial group, should be recommended.

Use of outside programs. Frequently a company will belong to a trade association or have links to an academic or professional group. The marketing plan needs to pinpoint the value of the connection, with a recommendation for continuation or change.

Not all of these support organizations and programs are used in all companies. However, this section of the marketing plan should not be thought of as a catch-all, to be used only after the key programs have been identified and the action plans for the coming year explained. Good support usually means good cooperation, and good cooperation is one of the signs of the market-oriented company.

10. Direction, appraisal, and development

Direction. Because there are many variables in a marketing operation, continuing and effective direction is essential. In the factory a machine can be set up for a specific job and periodic inspection will be all that is needed while the operation is repeated time after time. The marketing team, however, continually faces new situations. Problems need resolution, flagging spirits need lifting, and opportunities must be met with decisive action.

Appraisal. Great advances are the order of the day in techniques of recording performance and analyzing the causes of varying levels of achievement. Hopefully the marketing information system has already been tied to the company's accounting program and provides data quickly and correctly. The field manager's prime concern should be to make sure that his people are not reporters first and salesmen second.

Improvement. One problem with an annual marketing plan is that people are afraid to tinker with it, and so take the easy way out by deciding that next year's plan is the appropriate time and place for change. Corporate marketing channels must be wide open for the proposal and implementation of improvements. The production group does not hesitate to order an engineering change, even to the extent of declaring present inventory obsolete, when facing critical problems or opportunities. Marketing sometimes has a Micaw-berish air — everything will turn out fine when the year's results are in. Not so, and the marketing plan must insure that improvement follows swiftly after appraisal.

11. Planned revenue, expense and profit

In this final section of the marketing plan all the proposals are translated into financial terms. While some key figures may have been used in the opening statement of objectives, the details should be reserved until the individual programs, or the changes to be made in them, have been explained. Getting a marketing plan ap-proved is a sales exercise, and it is logical to explain the value of a product before turning to a full discussion of its price. Because marketing is so creative and its options endless, it must not be bound by arbitrary financial limits. Industry-average marketing costs, previous expenditures, and ratios to sales volume or to profit are pertinent comparatives but should not be the reason for de-ciding what the marketing budget will be. Just as the market-ori-ented company tells its customer to look at value, so must it speak to itself. The question is not the cost but the return. What profit is projected, does it seem attainable, and does it represent sound value? If so, buy it.

There are other benefits for the company if the marketing pro-jections are accurate and realistic. The production group can operate with all the obvious efficiencies that are the reward of planning the work and working the plan. Accounting becomes easier and more exact. Few things upset financial results more than major varia-tions in the number of units sold or the price realized. As automa-tion increases, an increasing amount of business expense is of a fixed and nonvariable nature and the burden must be prorated over the expected output. When sales fall short of a goal, heavy unab-sorbed costs can deal a staggering blow to profits.

Allocating Marketing Responsibilities

Preparing and issuing an 11-point marketing plan not only co-ordinates this key operating function, but also clarifies the alloca-tion of marketing responsibilities and authorities. If the company is a new one, the individuals who will decide what each part of the plan contains must be designated, and they then become responsible for performance. In the existing company, the decision to produce a comprehensive plan may also call for another look at who does what, and the exercise can be a useful one. Even if the individual feels that he is clear about his area of responsibility, it pays to make sure that everybody else sees it the same way. In the checklist at the end of this chapter there is a list of major marketing activities, and space to insert the name of the person who plans and directs each function.

Completing Phase 1

The field sales manager makes his contribution to the creation of a market-oriented company by developing a complete field sales program. It becomes part of the marketing plan, which in turn is one of the major components of the corporate profit plan. The step-by-step building of a sales plan is discussed in logical sequence in the following chapters. Before turning to his assignment, the sales manager may need clarification of some of the policies and programs of the company and of the marketing department. The checklist that follows is the first of a series designed to make it easy to analyze the present situation for each major activity. The format is the same throughout the book, and three ratings are used— "OK," "Needs some work," and "Key area for attention." These are really subjective judgments, and the person completing the checklist must make his own definition for each of the rating categories. A fourth classification, "Does not apply," makes it easy to exclude those subjects that are not pertinent. For each checklist it may also be necessary to add additional items or to modify the wording to fit the individual company situation. Ideally, the evaluation should be a joint effort by the sales manager and his boss, so that they can agree on the status of the key factors and on when any needed changes can be made.

TOPIC	OK	NEEDS SOME WORK	KEY AREA FOR ATTEN-TION	DOES NOT APPLY

Corporate Action

1. Clear statement of the company's business mission and its objectives. | ____ | ____ | ____ | ____ |

2. Definition of marketing, production, and financial strategies. | ____ | ____ | ____ | ____ |

3. Clear organization of functions and allocation of duties and powers among key corporate managers. | ____ | ____ | ____ | ____ |

4. Prompt and accurate periodic operating reports and analysis of major internal and environmental factors. | ____ | ____ | ____ | ____ |

5. Regular appraisal of performance and decisive exploitation of opportunities or correction of deficiencies. | ____ | ____ | ____ | ____ |

6. Approved company profit plan (see below for marketing component), including: | ____ | ____ | ____ | ____ |

7. Production plan | ____ | ____ | ____ | ____ |

8. Financial plan | ____ | ____ | ____ | ____ |

9. Personnel plan | ____ | ____ | ____ | ____ |

10. Research and development plan | ____ | ____ | ____ | ____ |

11. Administrative plan. | ____ | ____ | ____ | ____ |

Marketing Plan

Key objectives and responsibilities
Responsibility of _____

12. Definition of major marketing objectives for the next three years (or longer). | ____ | ____ | ____ | ____ |

13. Definition of specific one-year marketing objectives. | ____ | ____ | ____ | ____ |

14. Assignment of marketing responsibilities to named individuals, and agreement by all concerned on division of tasks and authority. | ____ | ____ | ____ | ____ |

Checklist No. 1
(Continued)

TOPIC	OK	NEEDS SOME WORK	KEY AREA FOR ATTEN- TION	DOES NOT APPLY
Market Definition and Appraisal				
Responsibility of _____				
15. Definition of the market segments that the company has decided to serve and of the full potential (geographic, customer, and product or service) that could be tapped.	___	___	___	___
16. Selection of which geographic areas the company marketing effort will cover.	___	___	___	___
17. Selection of the types and classes of customers to be served.	___	___	___	___
18. Selection of the categories of products or services to be offered.	___	___	___	___
19. Review of 15 through 18 to insure that 100% of the potential has been analyzed, and that cover or don't cover decisions have been made.	___	___	___	___
20. Measurement of the size of the market the company has chosen, analysis of buying motives and purchasing trends, and appraisal of current environmental conditions.	___	___	___	___
21. One-year forecast of total demand for the products or services the company offers, and in the segments it covers.	___	___	___	___
22. One-year forecast of company's market share and resulting sales volume.	___	___	___	___
Products or Services				
Responsibility of _____				
23. Within the categories established in 18, definition of the exact product or service mix to be offered.	___	___	___	___

Checklist No. 1
(Continued)

TOPIC	OK	NEEDS SOME WORK	KEY AREA FOR ATTEN-TION	DOES NOT APPLY
24. Development of new or improved products or services.	____	____	____	____
25. Monitoring and appraising sales performance of company and competitive products or services.	____	____	____	____

Prices and Terms of Sale
Responsibility of _____

26. Clear assignment of authority and responsibility for setting prices and terms of sale.	____	____	____	____
27. Establishment of financial guidelines to be used in setting and changing prices.	____	____	____	____
28. Timely and efficient issuance of prices and terms of sale.	____	____	____	____
29. Definition of procedure and authority regarding deviations from published prices and terms.	____	____	____	____

Merchandising Programs
Responsibility of _____

30. Planning and execution of the advertising program.	____	____	____	____
31. Planning and execution of the sales promotion program.	____	____	____	____
32. Planning and execution of the public relations program.	____	____	____	____
33. Planning and execution of the information program for employees and customers.	____	____	____	____

Field Sales Coverage
Responsibility of _____

Checklist No. 1
(Continued)

TOPIC	OK	NEEDS SOME WORK	KEY AREA FOR ATTEN-TION	DOES NOT APPLY

Field Selling Programs
Responsibility of _____

(Rating of effectiveness will be done
with checklist that follows Chapter 2.)

Physical Distribution
Responsibility of _____

34. Establishment of procedures for
coordinating production and sales volume, and maintaining effective inventory levels. ⎯⎯ ⎯⎯ ⎯⎯ ⎯⎯
35. Planning and execution of shipments from the factory. ⎯⎯ ⎯⎯ ⎯⎯ ⎯⎯
36. Planning and execution of the field
warehousing and distribution program. ⎯⎯ ⎯⎯ ⎯⎯ ⎯⎯

Support Organizations and Programs
Responsibility of _____

37. Planning and executing the program for marketing administration. ⎯⎯ ⎯⎯ ⎯⎯ ⎯⎯
38. Planning and executing programs
involving technical, service, and parts
supply functions. ⎯⎯ ⎯⎯ ⎯⎯ ⎯⎯
39. Planning and executing the personnel services program. ⎯⎯ ⎯⎯ ⎯⎯ ⎯⎯
40. Planning and executing credit and
collection programs and activities. ⎯⎯ ⎯⎯ ⎯⎯ ⎯⎯
41. Planning the effective use of outside programs and services and securing effective results. ⎯⎯ ⎯⎯ ⎯⎯ ⎯⎯

Checklist No. 1
(Continued)

	OK	NEEDS SOME WORK	KEY AREA FOR ATTEN- TION	DOES NOT APPLY
TOPIC				

Direction, Appraisal, and Improvement
Responsibility of _____

42. Continuous and effective leadership of all members of the marketing team. ⎯⎯ ⎯⎯ ⎯⎯ ⎯⎯

43. Appraisal of performance against plan and accurate reporting of marketing results. ⎯⎯ ⎯⎯ ⎯⎯ ⎯⎯

44. Establishment of effective and timely procedures for changing and improving programs, seizing opportunities, and overcoming obstacles. ⎯⎯ ⎯⎯ ⎯⎯ ⎯⎯

Planned Revenue, Expense and Profit
Responsibility of _____

45. Establishment of planned objectives covering all major categories, and including sales volume and price. ⎯⎯ ⎯⎯ ⎯⎯ ⎯⎯

46. Establishment of a consolidated marketing budget. ⎯⎯ ⎯⎯ ⎯⎯ ⎯⎯

2 / Major Components of a Field Sales Program

"GET out there and *sell!*"

It's a great challenge (or command) from the boss, and the field sales manager who is not thrilled by the chance to lead a group of men is probably in the wrong job. Aside from having the personal qualities that make him a good leader, what must a sales manager do to be the best in his league? He must do exactly the same as every other manager in his or any company: plan his program, organize his people, provide the tools, develop the skills, lead the team, and make effective changes for improved performance. This chapter is a brief summary of Phases 2 through 5 in the development of a field sales program. The following chapters expand on each major subject, with checklists, exhibits, and other examples.*

Phase 2
Planning and Organizing the Field Sales Effort

After the fundamental marketing, production, and financial strategies are decided, excellent parameters are established for the field sales effort. Working within them, the sales manager proceeds

* For a study of the field sales program from the viewpoint of the individual salesman, see *Managing a Sales Territory* by this author, American Management Association, 1971.

with the four components of Phase 2: He defines and measures the field sales task, formulates the customer and prospect coverage plan, sets the structure of his sales force, and determines its size and location. Planning and organizing—deciding what must be done and what will be available to do the job—are the first order of business. Certainly there will be continuing reappraisal as markets and products change, as competition makes moves, and as analysis provides greater insight into the company's opportunities and challenges. Nowhere is the need for unending improvement greater than in the field sales program.

Phase 2, Step 1
Defining and Measuring the Tasks

Indicating *tangible results* expected is the first task. Sales objectives, including the volume to be attained and the desired product mix, must be consistent with the company profit plan. Results in terms of the prices to be obtained and the planned selling costs should be forecast. The nonselling results expected also need definition, including assignments in administration, product development, technical service, and distribution.

Sales coverage results to be achieved involve a delineation of the geographic areas to be worked, and the types of customers and prospects to be served. The decisions must be based on company-wide analyses of the variables. It is wrong to cover a market so distant that freight and handling costs wipe out profit. It is equally wrong, however, to make that decision until finance has calculated the profit effect of the new sales that would result, or until production has explored the buying and assembly options that could give a lower landed cost.

Intangible results are by nature hard to define and even harder to measure. It is important, though, to agree on the amount of support the sales force is to provide for other departments, and on the image it should create in the minds of buyers and prospects.

Phase 2, Step 2
Formulating the Customer and Prospect Coverage Plan

Once the sales task has been defined, it become possible to establish a sound plan for field coverage. Information about customers and prospects must be collected and organized, so that the required sales effort is clear. The many accounts must be evaluated and classified to make sure that those that are important stand out prominently and to weed out those not worth sales effort. Finally, patterns of account coverage must be developed, specifying how much attention is to be given, based on value, location, and need. The format for specialized sales campaigns needs to be drawn up. Sales coverage policies cannot be left to the man in the territory; the company's program must set the guidelines that govern the nature and intensity of field sales work.

Phase 2, Step 3
Setting the Structure of the Sales Force

Many options are open in building the structure of the sales force. The basic decision is whether to use full-time company salesmen, or independent contractors such as agents or brokers, or a combination of both. The next decision is the allocation of products or services. Will each man sell the full line? If not, will the division be made according to product groups, markets, or technical skills needed for selling? Will all the customers and prospects in a geographic area be serviced by one salesman? If not, how will they be apportioned to insure full coverage without overlaps or voids.

When the organization of the first-line contact is settled, the method of supervision — directing, training, and motivating — usually becomes clear. The manager can decide whether he should organize geographically, with a branch manager in charge of all sales effort in a region, or have supervisors for specific products who operate throughout the company's marketing area. The administrative tasks, already defined, must be parceled out. Will they be done at the main office or in the field, and who will do them?

Phase 2, Step 4
Determining the Size and Location of the Sales Force

The final step in Phase 2 is to decide how many people are needed, where they will be located, and how much they will cost.

Several methods of analyses can help to make the decision about the size of the sales force a systematic one. There are no magic formulas, but there are measurement techniques that eliminate guesswork. As for location, it is being overoptimistic to think that every person will always be in the best market-oriented spot to do his job. By following tested principles, however, the manager can steadily improve the arrangement, perhaps not to perfection, but better than competition.

Phase 2 concludes with the establishment of a manning table and field sales budget. The sales, supervisory, and administrative functions can be accurately portrayed, together with the major cost items. Ratios can be calculated, comparing sales expense to other figures such as volume and profit. Following the steps in sequence produces a sound and dynamic plan that will insure enough effort, and the right kind of effort, to attain all the results expected.

Phase 3
Staffing, Training, and Motivating

Translating a manning table into a coordinated, skilled sales force is the next major phase. Guided by the sales coverage plans already established, the sales manager recruits his sales force. Inevitably he will find that the men he can attract do not possess all the skills needed for the job or that their performance level is below what he needs. A training program designed to produce the kind of salesman that the market wants must be created and made to work. In the final section of Phase 2 a powerful package of motivational forces is organized to make sure that those who can do the job will do it.

Phase 3, Step 1
Recruiting the Sales Force

An accurate definition of the need is the first step in recruiting a sales force. A sales profile or position guide is drawn up to spell out the responsibilities and duties of the salesman and to identify the skills he must have to serve his customers effectively. As the specifications for the sales force are resolved, the type of supervision that will be needed also becomes clear. Administrative and nonselling personnel will be required, and brief descriptions of their duties help to improve the selection process. Throughout the definition period, a wise sales manager encourages those who will do the work to participate in deciding how to go about it.

Finding and attracting candidates requires a measured program that uses multiple sources to let prospective employees know that job openings exist. The right kind of advertising can produce many replies from qualified candidates; the wrong advertising will bring too few and inadequately skilled applicants. The search is not always directed outside, and company employees are carefully screened for possible sales work. Selection, through skilled interviewing, checking, and testing, leads to the best candidate for the job. The recruiting process is completed with hiring, which includes the immediate definition of individual training activities and the setting of specific sales goals to be attained.

Phase 3, Step 2
Developing Skills

Training is a continuing need, but it must be concentrated on the key sales skills, and it must be done in a way that encourages rather than discourages the participation of those being trained. By whatever name called, the program must be based on the sales profiles or position guides already prepared. Its goal is to increase the ability of both present salesmen and new men to handle the four major components of their job. A wide choice of training methods is available.

Individual training starts with a basic standard package of information that enables all new men to understand the job and the company. Customized training is then designed to supply those skills needed when the salesman takes over his assignment. As he develops his territory program, his progress is carefully watched, and a continuing training program helps him become even more proficient at his many tasks. In all phases of individual training the participation of the salesman is insured by having him help decide, from the day he was hired, what new knowledge and abilities he needs and how he will acquire them.

Group training can be used to teach new skills or techniques, and for periodic review and stimulation. Much of what passes for sales training is so poorly organized and presented that it builds resentment among the better salesmen, who deplore the waste of their time. Proper definition of objectives, as explained in Chapter 8, can insure that pertinent material is created and then effectively communicated to the sales force. The complete training program must also include conscientious attention to the needs of supervisors and administrative employees.

Phase 3, Step 3
Motivating Superior Performance

It is not enough to find a salesman and train him; he must be incited to action if the results he produces are to be equal to the goals set for him. The keystone of a comprehensive motivational package is a sound compensation arrangement. The first component is either an equitable guaranteed income or commission arrangement. To be equitable, it must be based on an individual standard of performance, agreed to by both the sales manager and the salesman. The company benefit program, including insurance, retirement, and other safeguards, is then supplemented by additional privileges and perquisites. The total compensation plan motivates each man to achieve the results spelled out in his standard of performance.

Incentives and contests provide additional motivation, calling forth that extra and temporary surge of effort often needed to overcome a sales dip or to capitalize on a market opportunity. To be effective they must conform to tested principles; otherwise they lose their power or, even worse, reward the sales force for doing what is not the principal objective from the company viewpoint.

Even though a broad system of incentives has been designed, the motivation program is not complete if it does not provide for *career development*. Whether the individual salesman wants to be promoted to the managerial level or wishes to remain as a profitable and loyal territory salesman, the company must provide him with the rewards and recognition he needs. Only by doing so will it be able to retain its best men.

Phase 4
Creating Selling Programs

Each salesman must be equipped with selling materials and sales campaigns that support him on the call and that amplify the impact of his message; he must have visual aids, demonstrations, and proof of performance. Management has failed if it sends a man into the field to work unaided.

The creation of a selling program is Phase 4 in the development of a complete sales effort. It begins with an examination of the entire company merchandising effort, and then proceeds to the design of the specific materials and techniques that the men in the field will use.

Phase 4, Step 1
Designing the Merchandising Program

The basic objective in designing a merchandising program is to present a unified high-impact message that the buyer receives clearly and that impels him to take favorable action. It must be founded on a clear definition of who the buyer is and what he is looking for, not always as simple a task as it appears to be. The decision makers must be pinpointed, as there may be separate groups for each market segment, or even within one segment. Many purchases result from a series of actions by a number of interested people, and it is essential that the decision-making pattern be clear, so that the merchandising and selling effort can be addressed to the right people and in the correct sequence.

A buying decision is the result of progress through the steps of a purchase, but the prospect needs information and answers before he will move from his initial attention to the final action that produces a sale. Each seller must therefore analyze his decision makers and tabulate the kind of data that will be necessary to win the order. Although there appear to be many buying motives that influence the decision makers, they usually fall into a few major categories, and "What makes our customers buy?" is a question that everyone in the company needs to study and answer. Not every prospect buys what is offered, and the reasons that make him reject or postpone a favorable decision are the buying objections, usually valid ones, that must be answered if a sale is to be made.

Merchandising is more than salesmanship and advertising. For example, the customer will have definite ideas about delivery requirements. If his wishes are carried out, the opportunity for a sale rises sharply; ignore or oppose what he wants and he will buy from someone else. The final step in constructing the profile of those to whom the merchandising program is directed is to list the after-sale demands for such additional benefits as training, service, and warranty protection.

When the decision makers have been identified and their needs cataloged, the company can begin to develop its responses. It calls on all departments, not on marketing alone. The responsibility for communicating with the decision makers must be allocated to those best equipped to gain the prospect's attention and to speak to him in clear terms. Depending on whether the company sells to consumers or industry or government, the division of communication can take many forms. It must also conform to the customer's decision-making pattern, for many a sale has been lost by not addressing the various decision makers in the order they prefer and with the answers they need.

The steps of a sale are the same as the steps of a purchase, but they represent the seller's response to the customer needs that he has identified. Merchandising must insure progress through the five steps, whether the buyer is a new customer, a repeat account of many years' standing, or a secondary decision maker who supports the buying decision. The order must then be translated into a delivery and into after-sale care that brings a satisfied nod of approval from the purchaser.

Phase 4, Step 2
Providing the Selling Tools

Making successful sales calls is the key responsibility of the field force, and well-designed selling tools and sales campaigns are needed to make sure that the results the sales manager has pledged to attain are in fact achieved. The creation of a powerful program is aided by the care with which the company has delineated the whole merchandising task—the sales force knows who it must see and what it must do.

The manager starts by defining the principal types of sales calls his men will make. Each call is different, but it is also a variation on a handful of repetitive sales assignments that must be performed efficiently yet artistically. As he makes a call, a professionally competent salesman goes through eight specific activities to complete the calling cycle. His manager must study each of these parts of a call to determine what task is being performed and what information and equipment his men must have.

When this thorough analysis of all aspects of the sales call is complete, the selling aids and sales programs that are needed can be described. Every salesman must have the basic equipment that helps him to manage his territory efficiently, and to offer his products and services to many customers and prospects. This should be supplemented with individual territory aids that personalize the basic material and give it more local appeal.

In the early stages of building the sales program, the market segments in which the company operates were clarified, and now the decision must be made as to whether the standard equipment will be adequate for the sales task, or whether special material must be created for individual market segments. The final step in organizing the program is to make sure that the transportation and communication equipment provided for the men really does help them to create the maximum amount of selling time.

All the tools are then coordinated into a number of sales campaigns that help each salesman progress through a series of calls and interim objectives to the winning of a major sale. The building of a campaign is a substantial undertaking, and the manager enlists the support of his field force and his associates in the company in the complicated task of systematically linking a series of actions so that they produce one cumulative effect. Design and field testing takes a selling idea and translates it into a brochure, a presentation, or a visual aid. Too many companies skimp at this juncture, and what could be a dynamic merchandising tool turns out to be mediocre, unattractive, and unused. Instruction in using selling aids has already been incorporated in the training program that is underway, and the salesmen receive both initial and periodic coaching in how to get the most out of the tools the company has provided.

Phase 5
Leading, Appraising, and Improving

Having organized an efficient and comprehensive program, the sales manager must now provide the leadership that will stimulate his men, strengthen them in adversity, and help them make the most of their opportunities. He looks first at himself and candidly appraises his qualifications. He must have a number of business skills related to his products and markets, in addition to the professional skills of sales management and creative leadership. His own personal attributes need to be examined. If he must change himself, or develop new talents, he has an obligation to his company and to his men to set up his own training program.

Once satisfied that he is worthy of his title and his assignment, the effective manager can begin the process of leading, appraising, and improving his sales team. Appraisal must be based on facts, and he makes sure that an efficient system supplies him with prompt and accurate data. As he and his associates study the progress reports, they maintain a positive attitude and search for breakthroughs and opportunities; they don't look only for problems and the chance to criticize. When objective appraisal points to a change, the process of making improvements is carefully controlled. He is not an indecisive leader, but neither does he give fast answers to complicated problems.

The major control areas include the development of unit and territory selling programs that promote the idea that each man is a manager, not a worker, and must think and act like a manager. The sales manager also watches performance against plan. He checks to see that accounts are being called on as he wishes them to be and that the calls are truly successful ones that use the selling aids he has provided. Key customers often receive his personal attention, and he knows the status of these critical accounts. The decisions made about the size and structure of the sales force must be examined and reexamined, and changes will be needed to keep a lean team of fighting men who can hold up their share of the total marketing task.

Because he is a good sales manager, he knows the value of human relations. He watches the morale of the field force, assessing whether the motivational package he has created is doing its job. As part of this appraisal, he has established the best system he can devise to rate the performance of individual salesmen. This enables him to reward his best men and to make sure that they stay with him. Those men whose work is substandard receive special counseling and training, but if they do not measure up, he sees that they move off the sales team and that a better man steps in. In addition to his work with the men and women who report to him, the sales manager has important leadership responsibilities both within and outside the company. He must participate in the company-wide search for improvement by accurately reporting conditions in the field, and he must be the company's ambassador to many customer, academic, and industry groups.

Where Do We Go from Here?

This chapter has summarized all the many major actions that produce a complete field sales plan. In the following chapters each topic will be studied in more detail, and examples given to suggest ways of tackling that particular phase of the job. The question therefore is "Where do we go from here?" Should the sales manager begin at the beginning, defining or redefining his task and then proceeding through all the steps of a complete program development? Is one part of the sales effort so ripe for improvement, or so deficient, that it should be the first order of business? To assist in making this decision, the next checklist includes all the components of a comprehensive field sales program and allows the sales manager to rate the present level of performance. Only the man in charge can decide what the next move should be, and the appraisal that follows will help him make the best choice.

Checklist No. 2
The Major Components of a Field Sales Program

TOPIC	OK	NEEDS SOME WORK	KEY AREA FOR ATTEN- TION	DOES NOT APPLY
Phase 2: Planning and Organizing the Sales Effort				
Step 1: Defining and Measuring the Task				
1. The tangible results to be obtained by the sales force have been defined.	⸻	⸻	⸻	⸻
2. The sales coverage results to be obtained have been defined.	⸻	⸻	⸻	⸻
3. Any intangible results that can be defined have been clearly stated.	⸻	⸻	⸻	⸻
Step 2: Formulating the Customer and Prospect Coverage Plan				
4. Information about individual customers and prospects has been collected and is well organized.	⸻	⸻	⸻	⸻
5. All accounts have been evaluated and classified, and there is a clear picture of the size of the required sales effort.	⸻	⸻	⸻	⸻
6. Patterns of sales coverage for the major customer and prospect categories have been logically developed.	⸻	⸻	⸻	⸻
7. Formats for specialized sales campaigns aimed at valuable market segments and key accounts have been developed.	⸻	⸻	⸻	⸻
Step 3: Setting the Structure of the Sales Force				
8. The best type of sales force (company-paid, other, or combination) has been selected.	⸻	⸻	⸻	⸻

Checklist No. 2
(Continued)

TOPIC	OK	NEEDS SOME WORK	KEY AREA FOR ATTEN-TION	DOES NOT APPLY
9. The division of products and markets among the sales force has been carefully decided.	___	___	___	___
10. Geographic coverage by the sales force is complete, without overlap and without voids.	___	___	___	___
11. A supervisory structure has been developed that provides maximum support and direction for the salesmen.	___	___	___	___

Step 4: Determining the Size and Location of the Sales Force

TOPIC	OK	NEEDS SOME WORK	KEY AREA FOR ATTEN-TION	DOES NOT APPLY
12. The size of the sales force has been arrived at through careful analysis of several methods of determining sales coverage needs.	___	___	___	___
13. Salesmen, supervisors, and sales facilities are located in a way that makes for efficient operation.	___	___	___	___
14. A current manning table accurately shows the size and location of the sales force.	___	___	___	___
15. A complete sales budget has been prepared, approved, and is controlling our expenditures.	___	___	___	___

Phase 3: Staffing, Training, and Motivating

Step 1: Recruiting the Sales Force

TOPIC	OK	NEEDS SOME WORK	KEY AREA FOR ATTEN-TION	DOES NOT APPLY
16. The skills, experience, and personality traits needed by the sales force have been recorded in sales profiles or position guides.	___	___	___	___

Checklist No. 2
(Continued)

TOPIC	OK	NEEDS SOME WORK	KEY AREA FOR ATTEN-TION	DOES NOT APPLY
17. An organized recruiting program is producing qualified, interested candidates.	⸺	⸺	⸺	⸺
18. The selection process includes skilled interviewing, careful checking, and testing to find the best candidate.	⸺	⸺	⸺	⸺
19. The hiring procedure includes mutual agreement on duties, training programs, and territorial goals.	⸺	⸺	⸺	⸺

Step 2: Developing Skills

20. There is an organized program for individual training, including both initial and continuing development of knowledge and ability.	⸺	⸺	⸺	⸺
21. Group training is effectively teaching new skills and techniques and providing periodic review and stimulation.	⸺	⸺	⸺	⸺

Step 3: Motivating Superior Performance

22. A sound compensation package includes guaranteed or contingent income, a formal program of employee benefits, and appropriate privileges and perquisites.	⸺	⸺	⸺	⸺
23. Each salesman has an individual standard of performance and is encouraged to create new and better ways to do his job.	⸺	⸺	⸺	⸺
24. A program of incentives and contests is calling forth extra effort and stimulating exceptional performance.	⸺	⸺	⸺	⸺

25. Planned career development is help-

Checklist No. 2
(Continued)

TOPIC	OK	NEEDS SOME WORK	KEY AREA FOR ATTEN- TION	DOES NOT APPLY
ing to retain our best men and to provide them with the recognition and personal rewards each man seeks.	___	___	___	___

Phase 4: Creating Selling Programs
Step 1: Designing the Merchandising Program

26. A complete company merchandising program has been developed, and the field selling aids are a carefully integrated part of that total effort.

27. The decision makers, their decision-making patterns, and the information they need have been identified.

28. We know the principal buying motives and buying objections that influence our customers and prospects.

29. The responsibility for communicating with the decision makers has been properly allocated, and the sales force knows exactly what it must do.

30. Our coordinated merchandising program is tailored to fit all the facts about the decision makers, as listed in 27 and 28.

Step 2: Providing the Selling Tools

31. The principal types of sales calls made by our men have been defined, as well as the selling task that confronts them during each step of a call.

32. Each salesman has a complete set of selling tools, including basic selling

Checklist No. 2
(Continued)

TOPIC	OK	NEEDS SOME WORK	KEY AREA FOR ATTEN-TION	DOES NOT APPLY
equipment, individual territory sales aids, and special material for particular market segments.	⸺	⸺	⸺	⸺
33. Salesmen can create the maximum amount of selling time because they have the most efficient transportation and communication equipment we can provide.	⸺	⸺	⸺	⸺
34. Sales campaigns have been developed that help our men attain major sales goals by giving them a planned sequence of action and the tools to do the job well.	⸺	⸺	⸺	⸺
35. Our selling aids are carefully designed and field tested, and our men are trained in their use.	⸺	⸺	⸺	⸺

Phase 5: Leading, Appraising, and Improving

36. I have listed the skills and qualifications I need to be an effective sales manager, have candidly appraised myself, and have established a program to acquire or improve the skills I must have.	⸺	⸺	⸺	⸺
37. I regularly receive correct and up-to-date reports of progress in each major sales sector, and continuously appraise performance and make improvements.	⸺	⸺	⸺	⸺
38. I am in close touch with each sales activity, know what is going on, and am considered a participative leader by my men.	⸺	⸺	⸺	⸺

Checklist No. 2
(Continued)

TOPIC	OK	NEEDS SOME WORK	KEY AREA FOR ATTEN-TION	DOES NOT APPLY
39. I know the best men and the weakest men on the sales force, and periodic counseling helps every salesman do his best.	____	____	____	____
40. There is effective and harmonious cooperation between the sales force and all other departments.	____	____	____	____
41. I have excellent relations with customers, industry associates, and government or academic groups.	____	____	____	____

3 / Defining and Measuring the Field Sales Task

MOUNTAIN climbing has one attribute that many businesses sadly lack, and that is clarity. The mountain is there for all to see; it can be measured, studied, and there is no question whether the climbers have attained the summit or not. The team, the equipment, and the training can be almost as exactly analyzed. A proposed action either helps to reach the top or it does not, and it is in or out as a result. It is true that environmental factors such as storms create problems, but mountain climbing is a tough job made easier because it can be so exactly defined. Would that business were the same!

Well, it can be. In building a field sales program the first step is to define and measure the mountain from many angles, and to be sure that all mean the same thing when they talk about "the mountain." Spelling out the task must be a prelude to every other field sales action, and the three major categories needing resolution are the tangible results, the sales coverage results, and the intangible results. The wisdom of corporate planning and of making a marketing plan now becomes apparent. If the sales manager can identify what he is to sell, to whom, and where, he has in effect written the specifications for most of the remaining parts of his program.

Conversely, to attempt to organize a field effort without first establishing specific objectives is foolish and wasteful.

Tangible Results

Sales Volume

The definition of the key tangible result, sales volume, must be a joint effort of several departments in the company. One input starts at the territory level, and the sales manager must then bring the forecast up through his organization step by step until he has a consolidated and realistic opinion of what the people in the field say can be done. In the following pages several grids will be shown as examples of how tangible results can be portrayed. Each grid should be used throughout the sales force. Requiring each man and unit to develop an individual forecast insures that the company's plan is being carried out—by products, by geography, and by market segments. Reassurance from the field that all is well is fine, but nothing replaces a set of figures that spells out what will be done and bears the commitment of the man who will do it.

The estimates from the field are then blended with the forecasts made by other marketing groups and tested against the constraints the business faces. The projected sales volume may be beyond the company's productive capacity or its financial means, and selective pruning may be called for. The final result should be a grid showing planned sales volume by major product groups and by time periods. Later on, this same type of grid will be used to define accurately the customer coverage results that must be attained, but for now it is a simple recapitulation of the dollars or number of units that will be sold during the coming year. Exhibit 6 shows such a matrix for a metal products manufacturer. It cannot be finally approved until the other component of the forecast—price—is also reviewed. Profitless prosperity is as bad as high-margin stagnation, and the agreement on tangible results must specify not only how much is to be sold, but how much money the company will earn from those sales.

Selling Profit

It is true that the sales manager cannot be held accountable for company profits. He has no control over production expense or, in the complex organization, over the allocation of fixed costs that can radically alter the apparent profitability. It is equally true, however, that he can and should be held responsible for a selling profit. It is often stated as the amount or percentage of markup over an established cost. In a commodity business, perhaps the only realistic task that can be assigned is to obtain the same prices for the same

Exhibit 6. Planned sales volume by products and time periods ($000).

Period	Kitchen & Medicine Cabinets	Office Furniture	Vehicle Components	Power Lawn Mowers	Hot Water Heaters	Total
January	$ 100	$ 200	$ 480	$ 500	$ 250	$ 1,530
February	250	200	560	600	300	1,910
March	450	180	560	940	180	2,310
Subtotal First quarter	800	580	1,600	2,040	730	5,750
April	380	150	620	1,160	220	2,530
May	680	600	620	950	240	3,090
June	510	400	560	460	220	2,150
Subtotal Second quarter	1,570	1,150	1,800	2,570	680	7,770
July	530	400	90	—	370	1,390
August	300	160	310	—	290	1,060
September	220	40	620	—	280	1,160
Subtotal Third quarter	1,050	600	1,020	—	940	3,610
October	680	100	620	—	100	1,500
November	450	50	780	200	50	1,530
December	350	—	470	500	150	1,470
Subtotal Fourth quarter	1,480	150	1,870	700	300	4,500
Annual total	$4,900	$2,480	$6,290	$5,310	$2,650	$21,630

products as those being charged by competitors who offer the same customer services. When the selling profit has been defined, the two components, volume and price, can be examined and a decision reached. If it is an affirmative one, the sales manager is told, "You are doing a good job when you sell this number of items, during this period of time, and bring in this number of dollars." The mountain has been identified and everyone agrees on some of its features.

Field Selling Expense

The cost of obtaining the planned sales volume must ultimately be proposed and approved, but only when the complete program has been developed. Until all the decisions called for in Chapters 3 through 12 have been made, it is too early to put down figures. A complete, typical sales budget—giving the projected expenses for next year, the actual expenses for the current year, and the percentage of increase or decrease—might be subdivided as follows:

People
 Supervision, salaries
 Salesmen, salaries
 Clerical and administrative salaries
 Employee benefit programs, company's share of cost
 Salesmen's commissions and incentives
 Commissions to manufacturers' agents

Tools
 Rent, operating equipment, and supplies
 Recruiting and training programs
 Sales aids and selling programs

Actions
 Automobile expense
 Other travel costs
 Telephone and postage
 Business entertainment

One of the useful features of an organized sales budget is that it gives freedom of action to the manager within defined limits. He gains advance approval for merit increases in salary, for planned additions to the force, and for new facilities and sales programs. Deliberate study once a year will produce more effective cost control than a habit of making each decision only at the last moment, when emotions and the current state of the business may exert too much influence. Anyone who has tried to obtain a raise for a good man when the sales curve has temporarily turned down knows the problem. When his annual selling expense plan is approved, the manager can then implement it in his own way and with the timing that is best for him.

In all three categories — sales volume, selling profit, and selling expense — the data should be fully coordinated with the company's basic accounting system, and the sales manager should agree with the way the figures will be recorded and presented. One manager inherited an extensive computerized data bank in which all records had been compiled according to territory numbers. There was no tie to political divisions, such as counties, or to market structure, such as major metropolitan areas. Naturally territory boundaries changed and, to make matters worse, territory numbering methods had also changed. An enormous amount of information had been compiled, but was of no use. To make any accurate comparison between past and present performance, a manual recap of invoices was required. The problem could have been avoided had accounting and sales discussed and agreed on the information standards to be used.

Other Tangible Selling Results

Every sales program includes other key actions that need definition. Unless the result to be achieved can be exactly described and exactly measured it does not belong in the tangible category. If it belongs anywhere it should be grouped with the other intangible goals to be discussed later in this chapter. The categories listed below are specific and measurable results often expected of a sales force.

Market share. Caution is the watchword here. Many times the data for total industry sales are not matched exactly to the company's product groups, and an accurate assessment of market share becomes impossible. If a company makes only drill presses there is no point in comparing performance with total sales of metal-working equipment. In another case, what were thought to be industry figures did not include the sales of one large supplier, and any conclusions based on the inaccurate data made a perilous foundation for marketing decisions.

In addition to market share, tangible results can include objectives for expansion of the distribution system. If the top 100 retailers who could sell the company's products have been identified, it makes sense to aim to have a specific percentage of them carrying the company's line.

New customers. Few if any companies have 100 percent distribution, and the sales force must regularly bring in new customers. The establishment of a numerical goal helps to clarify the amount of time that should be devoted to prospecting. The target may be restricted to the same types of customers already served or could be based on moving into a new distribution channel or a new geographic area. Frequently the new account task will be related to a timetable, especially in seasonal businesses where there is a time to look for new business but also a time to concentrate exclusively on serving present accounts.

New products. Defining new product goals is automatic in a market-oriented company; the value of coordination is too obvious to be neglected. The field sales task can include introduction of a brand new product or the sale of an improved model to existing users. Another frequent assignment is to sell an established product to new customers who will use it for an entirely new application, a market expansion move that the chemicals producers have used frequently.

Key accounts. Most of the sales volume and profit will usually come from relatively few customers, sometimes called the 80/20, or double pyramid, effect. In making up the sales forecast it is undoubtedly necessary to predict the probable volume and profit to be derived from the biggest accounts on the company's books. Thus it may be wise to list as a tangible result the amount of business the sales force must produce from key individual customers. The category can even be broadened to include a few critically important prospects, identifying specific individual goals that supplement the overall task already defined under the new accounts heading.

Nonselling results. As the company divided the tasks among the various departments, the sales force probably got some that cannot be defined in terms of sales results. Because these duties usually involve interdepartmental cooperation, it pays to spell them out as a guide to the sales manager in staffing and training his team. Sometimes the home office handles invoicing for nearby areas, while remote branches are required to prepare their own. Where some products are bought from outside suppliers, the sales force is frequently charged with keeping track of sales, placing orders for merchandise, and even for insuring timely receipt and inspection.

Within the company, a program for new product development may call for the field force to help test the prototypes. While the degree of cooperation may appear too intangible to put numbers on, the sales manager should not give up too quickly. Better to sit down with research and define exactly the desired number of participating customers, the kinds of tests, and the reports that will be required. Chances are that a tight, effective program will result if a more specific task can be set than "to assist R&D in product development by obtaining field tests."

Physical distribution is another assignment often given to the field force, and accurate definition of the results expected will pay off when the time comes for setting the structure and size of the sales force.

Summary

The tangible results that have been defined represent the first step in the development of an efficient field sales force. Agreeing on goals helps insure that there will be enough sales effort to make the rest of the company's activities worthwhile, and that the goals that the man in the territory strives to attain are consistent with the overall profit plan. From this basic definition of results it is possible to make additional judgments, especially about the sales coverage that must be provided if the objectives are to be reached.

Sales Coverage Results

In the market-oriented company, sales coverage is everyone's concern, and not a decision for the marketing director, let alone the field sales manager. From the geographic aspect, there are many options needing investigation, including new plants, local assembly using key parts or ingredients from the main factory, or contract manufacture by someone else. The types and classes of customers to be served are also a matter of common interest. Knowing the market helps research and production serve it; knowing the research and production capabilities sharpens the search for new markets. And pervading all the expansion activities are the financial considerations. The days when the sales people were never really told the true cost (for fear they would give the product away) are over. Now the emphasis is on an organized look at the "available dollars," the money left over from each sale after direct costs have been covered. The sales manager should therefore seek and expect the cooperation of all in defining the four factors that influence sales coverage: geography, customers, prospects, and influence groups.

Geography

Outer limits. A timeworn story tells of the salesman who slapped a $100 bill on the ticket agent's counter and said, "Give me a ticket." When the agent asked the destination, our salesman replied with spirit, "Makes no difference, I've got customers everywhere." Theoretically a business has no outer limits to its sales coverage, provided the buyer will pay enough to make the transaction profitable. Reality, however, dictates that the company define its area of operation. But just as the sales volume result could not be assessed without also considering the prices to be obtained, so the geographic boundaries must be linked to the cost of coverage and the profits that result.

The first decision is whether to cover only the domestic market or to seek export business. Within the United States the outer limits of coverage should be extended as far as possible; more errors are made by working too small an area than in overreaching.

Intensity of coverage. Once the outer boundaries are established, uniform coverage may be the best sales plan, but more often than not there is a variation in the intensity of coverage. One company worked only the major metropolitan areas; experience indicated that it simply did not pay to try to cover the smaller markets. Many companies solve the problem by selling direct to customers in prime areas and using wholesalers, and therefore fewer company salesmen, for the remainder.

Companies whose products require high transportation expense will frequently carve out geographic areas around each plant or distribution point, leaving the rest of the country to competitors who are making the same distinction between profitable and unprofitable geography.

Expansion plans. As a company matures it may extend its geographic coverage. Frequently the initial area is based on the productive capacity of the plant or on intimate knowledge of the local market; when the first phase is successfully completed, new areas beckon. The decision to expand calls for an accompanying decision about the structure of the sales force. For example, far less of a financial commitment is required if the move into the export market is through an established agent rather than through a company operation, but the rate of growth may be slower.

The field sales plan should spell out the timing for any geographic expansion, even if that expansion is only an organized canvassing of a new sector to determine the potential.

Portraying geographic coverage. There is really no substitute for an up-to-date map to portray the areas to be worked and the intensity of coverage. If the plan is portrayed visually it also helps trigger the "why not?" discussion among department heads that increases the coverage and, therefore, the potential sales volume. Conversely, the company may be doggedly hanging on to an area it really should drop, and a map may highlight the problem. For example, coastal producers originally worked far inland, because there were no competitors with interior plants. Market growth has brought inland factories, able to serve local demand better and more profitably, but has the coastal producer realistically assessed the area he should cover?

Defining geographic objectives. Probably the simplest way to summarize the geographic coverage plan is to prepare another version of the grid already shown in Exhibit 6, but to substitute the major geographic areas for the time periods. Exhibit 7 shows such an arrangement. In this case the basis for the division is the regional grouping established by the Bureau of the Census, plus major export areas. The analysis can also be made in terms of the company's own interior boundary system, with branch headquarters locations used to identify the specific area. This summary of the results expected insures that the company has not been shut off from a market that it can profitably serve, and that the amount of sales to be gained in a particular area is consistent with the potential, with the planned advertising and promotion program, and with the company's growth objectives.

Customers and Prospects

Hand-in-hand with the geographic analysis, the definition of the customers and prospects to be served must be a top priority

Exhibit 7. Planned sales volume by products and geographic areas ($000).

Area	Kitchen & Medicine Cabinets	Office Furni- ture	Vehicle Compo- nents	Power Lawn Mowers	Hot Water Heaters	Total
Northeast region						
Middle Atlantic	$1,270	$ 520	$ 560	$1,180	–	$ 3,530
New England	420	220	–	430	–	1,070
Regional total	1,690	740	560	1,610	–	4,600
North Central region						
E. N. Central	1,350	710	2,970	930	$1,480	7,440
W. N. Central	510	480	840	810	–	2,640
Regional total	1,860	1,190	3,810	1,740	1,480	10,080
Southern region						
So. Atlantic	190	210	850	240	60	1,550
E. So. Central	270	340	290	140	210	1,250
W. So. Central	–	–	140	–	–	140
Regional total	460	550	1,280	380	270	2,940
Western region						
Mountain	160	–	–	430	40	630
Pacific	460	–	–	–	490	950
Regional total	620	–	–	430	530	1,580
U.S. total	4,630	2,480	5,650	4,160	2,280	19,200
Canada	160	–	–	840	120	1,120
Latin America	90	–	390	310	160	950
Europe	–	–	70	–	–	70
Other areas	20	–	180	–	90	290
Export total	270	–	640	1,150	370	2,430
All areas total	$4,900	$2,480	$6,290	$5,310	$2,650	$21,630

in the market-oriented company. The two basic considerations are the *type* of account (the market segment it belongs to or the business it is in) and the *class* (the economic function it performs, such as manufacturing, distributing, or consuming). Such phrases as electronics manufacturer, office supplies retailer, and automobile parts wholesaler accurately describe both the type and the class of customer.

Customer type. In describing the customer types to be serviced, the sales manager needs a set of definitions that will have the same meaning for all. Therefore he will be better off if he can use an established system. No doubt in working with others in the development of marketing plans he has already seen the value of standard definitions in securing industry and government data that can be related to the company's operation. The Standard Industrial Classification is only one example of a carefully thought out way to designate meaningful segments of economic activity. It lists hundreds of categories, and many companies find they can define their account types by listing the SIC numbers of the customers' activities. The SIC approach will not work for some: in theory the packaging and fastener manufacturers serve almost every market and therefore must define their customers more in terms of end use or application. In some cases, industry associations will agree on definitions of products or markets, and the nomenclature can be used to define customer types in terms that have a consistent meaning.

Customer class. Having said which types of customers it will serve, the sales force must define the class of customer, and there is usually more than one. Some businesses sell to people, others sell through people, many do both. An oil company can sell gasoline directly to large users and fertilizers directly to farmers, set up local petroleum jobbers to reach small users, and sell packaged products through a wholesale-retail distribution network.

Definitions of customer class are not always crystal clear, or universally adhered to; witness the use of wholesaler and factory outlet. The key factor in assigning the account to a class should be the type of service it will require. This service need affects the size and the training of the sales force, and is a key decision in the complex question, "How do we move our product from our plant to the ultimate user?"

Prospects. The sales coverage plan for new business will involve two major groups of prospects. The first group includes the same types and classes of accounts already defined in the customer coverage plan. If the company does business with 15 municipalities in a state, the remaining municipalities are obvious prospects that need identification and evaluation. When a product has broad appeal to retailers who are trying to combat shoplifting, then all retailers become prospects.

As part of its expansion program, the company may also be reaching for new markets, and the sales manager must define the sales coverage results he will produce, just as he outlined his program for geographic expansion. If during the coming year he must develop business with original equipment manufacturers, he needs to include this task in his definition of tangible results expected. Failure to do so will mean that he will lack the manpower and budget to penetrate the new market effectively, and the rest of the company's program will founder because of insufficient field sales work.

Defining account coverage results. The sales task has already been measured and defined by product groups, time periods, and major geographic areas (see Exhibits 6 and 7). A similar breakdown of the sales task by types and classes of accounts is the final step in making sure that the goals the sales manager is setting are correct and are in every way consistent with the rest of the company program. Exhibit 8 shows how the same total sales volume used in the other examples is distributed among the customers the company already has and the prospects it hopes to convert during the coming year. The headings can be varied to suit the individual business, and some categories may have to be invented to describe accurately the marketing opportunities the company intends to exploit.

Are We Working the Full Potential?

When the three grids have been completed the sales manager has defined his task accurately and can again reflect on the eternal question, "Are we working the full potential?" There are always opportunities to extend the number of market segments, and thereby broaden the base on which the company's sales are built. One approach is to look through the descriptions in the Standard Industrial

Classification book, seeking businesses close in type to those now being sold and yet for some reason not now covered. If the company has built its distribution predominantly through wholesalers, what can it do to reach more classes of accounts, to call on and sell manufacturers, retailers, and large consumers?

Whatever the outcome of the study, the sales manager never takes independent action, but works closely with other company units. He realizes that the move to a new market segment is not just a matter of knocking on doors, but of presenting a complete market package and of being sure that the profit potential justifies the effort.

Secondary Buying and Influence Groups

In addition to those who do the buying, or participate in the buying decision, the sales force can be assigned to cover secondary

Exhibit 8. Planned sales volume by type and class of customer ($000).

Type of Customer	Original Equipment Manufacturers	Wholesalers and Jobbers	Retailers Sold Direct	Users Sold Direct	Total
Motor vehicle industry	$4,200	$2,090			$ 6,290
Mobile and manufactured homes	1,060				1,060
Builders and building supply				$ 840	840
Furniture and fixtures users and merchants		1,080	$ 920	120	2,120
Hospital and laboratory equipment users and merchants			160	720	880
Hardware, plumbing, and garden supply		6,320	4,120		10,440
Total	$5,260	$9,490	$5,200	$1,680	$21,630

influence groups. In the sale of building materials, for example, it may be wise to make sure that municipal officials are informed about the product and its conformity with local regulations. Agricultural chemicals often need extensive sales support work with colleges and state experiment stations. The line between a primary and secondary influence is not always clear. The manufacturer of building materials may call on architects even though he sells only to contractors, because he knows that in many cases the architect specifies what is to be used. Is the architect a primary or secondary influence? The answer is not so important as is making sure that the architect is covered—and according to defined standards that will be established when the customer and prospect selling plan is developed.

The type of coverage to be given secondary groups needs definition for two reasons: to prevent boondoggling and to insure that vital influences are not lost. Because direct sales may not result it will be hard to appraise the effectiveness of this sales effort. The man in the field can spend far too much time in the pleasant atmosphere of missionary work, avoiding the confrontation with customers and prospects who might refuse an order. At the other extreme, too much emphasis on short-term results may hurt in the long run. If those who can influence sales are listening only to the competitor as he tells about his improvements in products and services, this lack of coverage will eventually hurt the company that neglects the secondary buying group.

Intangible Results

By its very definition, an intangible result calls for a subjective, arguable statement of opinion as to whether or not the goal was reached. If the result could be measured, if it were factual, it would have been spelled out as one of the tangible results the sales manager is expected to attain. Because of its hazy aspect, an intangible result is often never reduced to writing and the opportunity for misunderstanding is increased. Despite the problems involved, it is still better to discuss the activities listed below and get top-level agreement on a definition than to leave the establishment of performance standards up to an individual far down the organization ladder.

Merchandising. The sales force undoubtedly has some responsibility in making the merchandising program effective. At the least, it may involve no more than furnishing a current list of customers and prospects for a direct mail program. At the other extreme the field force may organize local campaigns, including tie-in advertisements, displays, and local publicity. How should the merchandising role of this one sales force be defined? What does it have to accomplish to be doing a good job?

Training and technical service. Field sales forces are often assigned a training function, principally because they already know the product and they are on the scene; it can be an efficient arrangement. Where the product involves servicing and repair, the salesman must often be capable of intelligent diagnosis of trouble and of making simple repairs. Problems arise when the level of training and technical assistance to be provided has not been defined. Even in the best run organization there will still be an argument about whether the man in the field should have handled the job, or whether the expert from the factory really had to make the long trip. The real goal, of course, is to have happy customers, and that comes about through advance definition of responsibilities for the sales force and the technical group.

Other marketing activities. Market surveys and trade shows are only two examples of other types of marketing activity that can involve the field sales force. Without wanting to appear selfish, the sales manager will attempt to define the amount and type of support he must render so that he can organize his team properly.

Image. Trying to make a salesman conform too closely to an image has given birth to the many stories about mustaches, socks, suit colors, and the limbo that awaits those who failed to project the right image. Such humor illustrates how a sound idea can be carried too far. Today's company is concerned about what people think, and few of its employees have more impact on the opinions of others than the field salesman. The sales manager must define the image his salesmen should try to project, and it should be more enlightening than the often-found one of "creating the best possible image for the company in the eyes of customers and prospects." One company dealing with small-town merchants and farmers encourages its men to involve themselves in community work, plays down its own corporate name, and fosters the image of a man in business for himself and doing business with neighbors. Just as important for another company selling commodities is that their men create the image of the good life, necessitating club memberships, high expense accounts, and frequent entertainment. Spelling out the image gives the man in the field the confidence and the guidelines he needs. In all probability he is in his present job because he likes it, but he will like it even more when he knows that what he is doing is exactly what the company wants him to do.

Defining the Complete Task

All of the key sales tasks have now been examined, and many of them measured and defined. Frequently one option will have to be compared carefully with another (volume to price, geographic coverage to selling cost) before the best solution can be found. In some cases, as for example with sales budgets, a complete definition must wait until all the components of the program are established and unified. The following checklist, arranged in the same sequence used in this chapter, can help the sales manager make sure that he has defined everything necessary for a clear understanding of his assignment. Once he secures the concurrence of his superior, he can proceed to the second step of Phase 2, the formulation of the customer and prospect coverage plan.

Checklist No. 3
Defining and Measuring the Field Sales Task

TOPIC	OK	NEEDS SOME WORK	KEY AREA FOR ATTEN- TION	DOES NOT APPLY

Tangible Results Expected

1. Sales volume goals have been established in terms of major products and time periods (see Exhibit 6).

2. The goals are realistic and are based on a careful analysis of field estimates, other forecasts, and business constraints.

3. The selling profit to be attained has been defined in measurable terms.

4. The field sales budget has been accurately defined, or it will be when a complete sales program has been established.

5. The sales information system is organized to provide prompt and accurate reports of performance against the sales goals.

6. Goals for market share or for percentage of distribution effectiveness have been established, and progress can be accurately measured.

7. We have established as a goal the number of new customers to be won in our present market segments.

8. For those new market segments now added to our sales effort, the number of new customers to be obtained has also been defined.

9. The specific results to be achieved in the sale of new products have been clearly stated.

10. Where possible, annual goals have been set for our sales to key customers and prospects.

Checklist No. 3
(Continued)

TOPIC	OK	NEEDS SOME WORK	KEY AREA FOR ATTEN- TION	DOES NOT APPLY
11. All tangible nonselling tasks have been defined in writing, and the results to be obtained are equally clear.	___	___	___	___

Sales Coverage Results Expected

12. The outer limits of the geographic area that is to receive coverage have been defined.	___	___	___	___
13. Sound and careful decisions have been made about the specific interior geographic areas to be worked, and about the intensity of sales coverage to be provided.	___	___	___	___
14. There is a plan and timetable for the expansion of field sales coverage and they fit the company's program for moving into new markets.	___	___	___	___
15. An up-to-date map accurately portrays the sales coverage plan.	___	___	___	___
16. Geographic sales objectives have been summarized by showing sales or profit goals according to significant areas and products or time periods (see Exhibit 7).	___	___	___	___
17. All present market segments have been studied, and the types of customers and prospects to be called on have been defined.	___	___	___	___
18. The classes (economic function categories) to be served have also been defined.	___	___	___	___
19. In addition to present customer and prospect sales effort, there is a plan for				

Checklist No. 3
(Continued)

TOPIC	OK	NEEDS SOME WORK	KEY AREA FOR ATTEN- TION	DOES NOT APPLY
expanding sales coverage to new types and classes of accounts that are not now being covered.	⎯	⎯	⎯	⎯
20. The planned sales goals have been defined for each major type and class of account and there is an accurate picture of sales coverage results expected (see Exhibit 8).	⎯	⎯	⎯	⎯
21. The complete sales coverage plan has been analyzed to make sure that the full market potential worth covering is in fact being covered.	⎯	⎯	⎯	⎯
22. Secondary buying and influence groups have been defined, and their needs in terms of information and service are clear.	⎯	⎯	⎯	⎯
23. A sales coverage program that provides appropriate coverage of secondary buying and influence groups has been established.	⎯	⎯	⎯	⎯
Intangible Results Expected				
24. The merchandising responsibilities of the sales force have been defined.	⎯	⎯	⎯	⎯
25. All training and technical service duties assigned to the field sales group are clearly stated.	⎯	⎯	⎯	⎯
26. The results expected in the fields of market analysis, trade shows, and other support functions have been established.	⎯	⎯	⎯	⎯
27. There is an accurate definition of the image the sales force is expected to create.	⎯	⎯	⎯	⎯

4 / Formulating the Customer and Prospect Coverage Plan

LACK of follow-through all the way to the individual call is the downfall of many sales programs. The company has systematically developed its products to appeal to its market segments, and its manufacturing, administrative, and distributing activities are efficiently organized. It may even have done a good job of recruiting and training its field sales force. But then the direction and the control disappear. The man in the territory is left to his own devices, frequently making his own decisions about where to call, how often to see each account, and what to do when he gets there.

This management failure can usually be traced to a lack of knowledge, not only about the customers and prospects, but also about what a field sales coverage plan should involve. When he formulates his plan, the sales manager has five objectives, in this order of importance:

Maintain present sales and profits. The company's most valuable marketing asset is the steady flow of cash from its existing business, and the first concern of the field sales program must be to preserve that revenue as the base on which plans for growth can be founded.

Increase business with present customers. Each salesman should look first to his current accounts for more volume. They already know him, do business with him, and like what he sells; they are the best prospects he has.

Win new accounts in present market segments. The company has developed a successful sales program that already appeals to specific types and classes of customers. The best new account candidate is one that has the same needs and buying motives as existing accounts.

Expand into new markets. When the first three objectives have been covered by the sales program, it is time to turn to the more difficult task of breaking into new markets. Here is where management direction and control are vital if the field sales force is to hold up its share of the total company growth program.

Regain lost customers. Where there once was harmony there is now a void; someone who at one time bought the company's product or services no longer is a customer. The sales coverage plan must therefore provide for regular assessment of lost accounts, remedial action where needed, and a continuing effort to resume shipments.

These objectives can be attained if a comprehensive plan is organized and if the sales force is required to carry it out. The aim is not to stifle individual initiative, but to encourage it within an orderly framework that the sales manager has defined. The steps in developing customer and prospect coverage follow a logical pattern:

- Collecting and organizing information
- Evaluating and classifying accounts
- Establishing planned sales coverage
- Developing skills through training
- Creating selling programs
- Recording and appraising group and individual performance
- Supervising, counseling, retraining

This chapter deals with the first three actions, those that establish the principles of the sales coverage plan. Later chapters describe how training, selling programs, performance appraisal, and periodic counseling make sure that the coverage does take place as scheduled and is effective in increasing sales and profit.

Collecting and Organizing Information

Any intelligent sales plan is so dependent on accurate information about customers and prospects that it will be assumed an effective sales reporting system already exists. Leadership must be based on knowledge of the situation, although many companies have never adequately analyzed their market segments. One corporation with 17,000 accounts did not know which were its 100 most profitable customers, had no accurate idea about its market share in many states, and had no information about individual customers other than name and volume. Organized data about prospects and lost accounts were nonexistent. Of course, a great deal was known at the branch level, but the corporate managers, particularly those who had joined recently, were operating in the dark—and the company was over 50 years old. Proof, possibly, that you don't have to know it all, but chances are the company would have been even bigger and more profitable had there been good information for decision making.

Information About Present Customers

There are five categories of customer information needed by the sales manager:

1. *Actual sales to the account.* An essential tool is a consolidated customer list, ranking accounts from largest to smallest, perhaps with an "all other" grouping below a certain size.

2. *Actual profits on sales to the account.* The same kind of list, ranking customers from the most profitable on down, is more meaningful than one that shows volume alone, but often much more difficult to obtain. Profitability lists frequently suffer from a large credibility gap.

3. *Potential for growth.* Knowing which customers offer the greatest opportunity for increased sales is essential for effective sales direction.

4. *Customer category.* The sales reporting system should be able to separate sales or profits by the industry served, the class of trade, or the end use.

5. *Geographic divisions.* The origin of sales profits by states, metropolitan markets, or company-designated regions is an indicator of success and of needed action.

Information About Prospects

The man in the territory is often the most competent source for information about prospects. Especially if the company's sales effort is reasonably mature, there is usually a deeper reason than lack of sales coverage that makes an account buy from a competitor. And that reason is as important to know as some of the figures about consumption and future potential. Others in the company may contend that the field salesman is exactly the wrong man to provide prospect information, since he will defend his own sales performance and will report biased or incomplete data. The sales manager with that kind of a sales force has far deeper problems than its competence in market survey work.

Prospect information must be developed not only for unsold accounts in present market segments, but also for the entirely new markets the company intends to enter. The major categories needing clarification are:

- Total current consumption
- Probable future consumption at *x* date
- Present suppliers and, if possible, prices paid
- Realistic chances of selling the account

Information About Lost Customers

When is a customer "lost"? For the manufacturer of large cranes, a three-year interval between sales to an account may cause less concern than a ten-day lapse of business between a printer and a large advertising agency that places orders daily. "Lost" can mean lost permanently, as when a customer starts to make what he formerly bought, or lost only until some temporary problem is solved. The definition must be clear, and the sales reporting system must provide the manager with a periodically updated list of those who no longer buy. Without an organized procedure it is certain that customers who could be won back will be left alone too long. The salesman will rarely publicize his lack of business, and unless the parting was a stormy one, the customer will be silent.

Organizing Customer and Prospect Information

There is usually an established method of periodically reporting sales to customers, and the sales manager will concern himself principally with changes needed to make the data more meaningful and less burdensome for him. He needs summaries, not pounds of printouts. Information on customer profitability can be incorporated in the same report. If actual profits cannot be calculated, then sales of premium-priced categories or the use of profit margins from previous years (in a nonvolatile industry) can indicate those customers who need the most attention. The organization of prospect and lost-customer information calls for a custom-made blend of what needs to be known and what can be found out. Key facts must stand out and not be lost in a mass of statistics.

The total output of the entire information process must be a summary of important data about the three major account groups: present customers, potential purchasers, and lost business. With the facts arranged in orderly fashion, the next step in developing sales coverage follows in logical sequence.

Evaluating and Classifying Accounts

All profitable customers are valuable but some are more valuable than others. Most customers have a growth potential but some grow more rapidly or are more easily served. Prospects and lost customers range from those who almost literally must be won to those not worth the effort. Evaluation and classification is needed not so much to prove what has been done in the past, but to improve what will be done in the future. The individual salesman must be given guidance about the frequency of sales coverage and the type of sales calls he should make.

Classifying present customers. Key accounts can usually be defined as those that have a major effect on the company's volume or profit. However, how much is a "major effect"? At the other end of the spectrum certain accounts are unprofitable, but does "unprofitable" mean in comparison with full factory cost, with incremental or direct cost, or with all costs plus average profit markup? In between the key and the unprofitable categories are the regular customers, the bulwark of the business. In establishing account classifications, the customer's potential is also a factor. The definitions of customer value should be kept simple, and the minimum standards for a key account should be high, as these are the buyers that need, and deserve, individually tailored sales programs and management attention. For example, one company set the following guidelines:

Key account: (a) Buys at least $250,000 from us annually *or*
(b) Has a total annual requirement of at least $500,000 for products made by us.

Unprofitable account: (a) Buys less than $5,000 annually from us *and*
(b) Has a total annual requirement of less than $25,000 for products made by us.

Regular account: All other customers.

Rating prospective customers. While the account's potential purchases are a key indicator in evaluating new customer prospects, other factors may be of even more importance in deciding how much sales effort should be applied. Establishment of a rating system, perhaps on a scale of 1 to 10, lets the sales manager control the broad type of coverage to be given to prospects. As with customer classification, the procedure should not be cumbersome. A chart such as Exhibit 9 can help to standardize definitions and eliminate such loose terms as "hot," "worthwhile," and "worthless."

Evaluating former customers. From the manager's standpoint, the coverage plan for lost customers should be a "go or no-go" measurement of several factors, including the account's potential, the reasons why the customer was lost, and the realistic chances of resuming shipments. Having already set up guidelines for account value, he can use them to help control the efforts of his salesmen, as for example:

Lost accounts that must be covered
    Potential equal to regular or key account, *and*
    No insuperable reason for loss, *and*
    Good chance of selling because problem has been or will be
    solved.

Exhibit 9. Prospect rating chart.

Account Name _____			
Location _____			
		Rating	
Category	2	1	0
Potential contribution to sales and profits	Equal to a key account	Equal to a regular account	Unknown, or too low
Financial condition, supplier relations and price policy	Financially strong, stays with supplier, buys value	Buys competitively, will shift sources easily	Unknown, or very unstable
Chances of selling the account	We have an advantage over competition	We are on equal footing	Unknown, or major problems
Our knowledge of the account	Have all the data needed	Some data, but not all	Little or none
Status of sales effort	Complete campaign in progress	In contact, program incomplete	No contact

Rating and date

_____

_____

_____

Lost accounts that may not be called on
    Potential below that of regular account, *or*
    Reason for not selling still applies, *or*
    Little or no chance of selling because problem cannot or will not
        be solved.

Consolidating Customer and Prospect Data

All the information and judgments made about the customers
and prospects need to be summarized into efficient working tools
that the sales manager can use in setting up his coverage plan for
the many kinds of accounts and the major market segments. He
must be able to pinpoint certain industries, patterns of use, and
types of customers. The sales effort needs to be focused on specific
levels of the distribution chain and restricted to defined geographic areas. Exhibit 10 shows a method of cataloging customers

Exhibit 10. A summary of information about customers and prospects.

	North Central Region		
Type and Class of Account	Key Customers	Regular Customers	Major Prospects and Lost Accounts
Hardware, plumbing and garden supply			
Manufacturer	4	14	21
Wholesaler	3	11	19
Retailer	2	163	284
Motor vehicle industry			
Manufacturer	3	2	2
Wholesaler	–	14	31
Furniture and fixtures			
Wholesalers	1	9	6
Retailers	8	49	62
Users sold direct	–	12	37
Total	21	274	462

and prospects. Even when the exact number of accounts may not be known, some indication of size is usually possible. When a clear picture of the required sales coverage emerges, the principles of the sales coverage plan can then be systematically defined. The control of the company's selling effort is where it should be — in the hands of the sales manager.

Establishing Planned Sales Coverage

In establishing the sales coverage plan the objective must be to insure *enough* sales effort, not merely a minimum or adequate coverage. Later on, as he decides on the size of his sales force and tests the realism of his budget, the sales manager may have to whittle here and cut there, but not now. There is no point in calling on an account unless there is a commitment to spend the time needed to win and hold it. Too often a salesman will be stretched over an impossibly large territory or customer group. He finds that he lacks time to serve his present accounts adequately and that new customer development never gets the follow-through it deserves. And yet, the company has zeroed in on specific market segments and is concentrating its resources. The sales force must do the same.

Measuring the Correct Sales Effort

Trying to establish patterns of sales effort is not easy. Each account is different in some way from all others, and to clamp too tight a lid on initiative means the sales force will be composed of territory workers, not territory managers. Until some rules are established, however, there is no way to check the adequacy of present sales coverage or to provide the type and number of men needed for additional field effort. Two ways of handling the problem are:

Establishing annual needs. Suppose the company sells a large part of its output through wholesalers. Even allowing for variations in accounts and salesmen, a typical pattern of sales and service needs can be established:

Type of Selling Effort	Frequency	Dura-tion	Annual Hours
Presentation of summer and winter product groups	2 per year	3	6
Regular planned sales cover-age	Biweekly	1/2	13
Group training of whole-saler's salesmen	2 per year	2	4
Field work with individual salesmen	Irregular	25	25
Total selling hours			48

From such an analysis it is clear that about 50 hours of person-to-person sales effort is needed if the wholesaler is to be properly informed, trained, and motivated. To do less defeats the concept of the market-oriented company. Spending a great deal more than 50 hours calls for justification because of account size, stage of development, or competitive pressures. The central sales coverage plan now provides meaningful guidelines within which the terri-tory manager can effectively serve each individual account.

Establishing call frequency. There are instances where the frequency of call can be defined, usually when the relationship with the account is fairly simple. A manufacturer of soap products may find that a large hotel can be efficiently served with three calls a year on the purchasing agent, combined with service checks every six weeks with the housekeeper. At the other extreme, no frequency standards can be set for the salesman of engineered fasteners who works with the development and test group of a major manufacturer; an individual sales plan must be set up.

In an established and repetitive sales coverage system, there-fore, it may be possible to divide accounts into a few major classes and to indicate the approximate interval between calls:

Type of Account	Call Frequency	Probable Annual Selling Hours
Key customer	Weekly	40
Regular customer, Class 1; or key prospect	Biweekly	20
Regular customer, Class 2; or regular prospect	Monthly	10

Defining Market Segment Coverage

The division of accounts among the several supply and demand market segments calls for the creation of sales campaigns that are appropriate to the need and the potential. A move into a new market will mean heavy selling effort for the coming year, far more than will be given to an established sector with consistent demand and little competitive pressure. Major decisions can now be intelligently made, based on the information summaries already completed.

Demand characteristics. Geographic coverage is a key demand factor. The account summary in Exhibit 10 listed about 750 accounts in the North Central region. If the Western region has only 140 accounts it will need less coverage (and perhaps a different sales force, as discussed in the next chapter). Within the region, there may be wide swings in demand that affect the geographic plan.

Supply characteristics. What sales coverage plan is logical for the products or services the company offers? Trucks are not sold on a house-to-house basis; antifreeze is sold in carload lots as well as a gallon at a time. What class of account is being served, and what kind of sales campaign is best? If the company is bringing a new regional plant into production, the sales coverage plan probably includes an intensive program that covers all potential users and involves individual calls, group meetings, plant visits, and work with secondary and buying and influence groups.

Intensity. The field sales effort must be related in intensity to the needs of the business and the customer. An industry switching from a chronic long-delivery schedule to an oversupply situation needs to increase its sales effort, and to begin that increase long before inventory starts piling up. If sales potential is booming, or substitute materials are making inroads (all part of the marketing plan's facts and figures), sales coverage must be stepped up. On the other hand, once regional distribution has been established for a new product, the intensity of coverage can probably be reduced and some of the salesmen reassigned to other markets.

All three factors—demand, supply, and intensity—are evaluated and a plan for sales campaigns evolves. The sales manager's final step in formulating his coverage plan is to make sure that he has set up a procedure for the nonselling tasks his men must perform, and that he has provided them with the time and tools for efficient territory management.

Organizing Other Duties

Nonselling assignments. The total task of the sales force has already been defined (Chapter 3), and it usually includes some responsibilities over and above making sales calls. Whether these duties are *selling* or *nonselling* is not important (and sometimes hard to decide, as with warehouse supervision). What is essential is that they be performed as the sales manager wishes, and not according to the individual territory manager. If the man in the field is to take periodic inventory of company and customer stocks, he must be told how to do it and the tools he needs must be provided. Sometimes the field force will have a major function in the field testing of improved products, and guidelines must be established so that manpower is available. If the nonselling assignments are not carefully included in the sales coverage plan, the inevitable result is that these peripheral duties will somehow get done and the person-to-person sales effort will suffer.

Territory management. In creating a market-oriented company, we defined one of the major corporate actions as: "Developing a decision-making process based on facts and figures." The need for scientific management is equally strong at the level of the individual sales territory. The sales manager has set broad guidelines for sales coverage, but he wants his men to interpret them in a way that provides maximum sales effort for local conditions. Facts and figures must be available, and the territory manager must have time to make his plans and submit them for approval. Too slavish a following of management guidelines will mean that excessive time is being spent with some customers while excellent prospects are neglected. Too little time spent in planning defeats the whole concept of measured sales effort.

The first requirement, therefore, is a system for furnishing sales information quickly to each man. Many companies already do this efficiently and in a way that does not require extensive record keeping in the field. Periodic reports required from the salesman need careful analysis. Why are they required, and is there no better way to get the information? One tested principle is to organize a salesman's paperwork on the basis that the company does not want any reports for its own use. All it wants is a copy of the reports the man in the field needs for efficient territory management. When measured against this criterion, paperwork assignments usually become far more realistic and are completed promptly and accurately.

Summary

The development of Step 2 of Phase 2 has now been completed. Information about customer and prospects has been collected and evaluated. There is a clear picture of the size of the sales task and the major categories of sales effort that are needed. Guidelines have been established for the amount and type of sales coverage to be given the principal account groups. The geographic emphasis, the special programs, and the supply and demand characteristics of the market have been taken into consideration. Ample time has been set aside for the nonselling tasks, and the territory managers will have the opportunity to plan their work and to act as true managers of their territories. To satisfy himself that his plan includes all the features he wants, the sales manager can complete the following checklist and then turn to Step 3 of Phase 2: setting the structure of the sales force that will carry out his coverage plan.

Checklist No. 4

Formulating the Customer and Prospect Coverage Plan

TOPIC	OK	NEEDS SOME WORK	KEY AREA FOR ATTEN- TION	DOES NOT APPLY
Collecting and Organizing Information				
1. We regularly and correctly report the sales made to each customer and the resulting profits.	___	___	___	___
2. We periodically prepare consolidated customer lists, ranking accounts in order of sales made to them, the profits earned by the company, and the total potential or annual requirements.	___	___	___	___
3. Our customers have been grouped according to geographic areas and market segments; we know the sales revenue and profit for each major category.	___	___	___	___
4. We have an organized procedure for collecting and recording information about new account prospects in the market segments we are already serving.	___	___	___	___
5. The new market segments that the company plans to enter are clearly defined, and we know what duties have been given to the sales force in the overall market development plan.	___	___	___	___
6. We are efficiently collecting data about prospects in new market segments, and we pass our information to other company departments.	___	___	___	___
7. We are receiving from other company departments the information they are developing about prospects in new market segments.	___	___	___	___
8. The definition of a lost customer is clear, and regular reports identify those accounts that have stopped buying.	___	___	___	___

Checklist No. 4
(Continued)

TOPIC	OK	NEEDS SOME WORK	KEY AREA FOR ATTEN-TION	DOES NOT APPLY

Evaluating and Classifying Accounts

9. Definitions have been established for key, regular, and unprofitable customers, and all accounts have been classified accordingly. _____ _____ _____ _____

10. A method has been developed that rates prospects according to their value and the chances of selling them, and a list of major prospects is kept current. _____ _____ _____ _____

11. A regular evaluation is made to determine which former customers can realistically be expected to buy again, and an up-to-date list is maintained. _____ _____ _____ _____

12. All the actions listed in 1 through 11 have been coordinated and we have a clear and complete picture of our customers, prospects, and lost accounts. _____ _____ _____ _____

Establishing Planned Sales Coverage

13. Our basic sales coverage plan is sound and our selling effort to customers and prospects is consistent with the company's marketing strategy. _____ _____ _____ _____

14. Guidelines have been established that indicate the typical annual sales coverage plan for each major type of customer. _____ _____ _____ _____

15. Where logical to do so, call-frequency patterns have been established to guide the salesman's effort. _____ _____ _____ _____

16. The major market segments have been analyzed and our sales coverage

Checklist No. 4
(Continued)

TOPIC	OK	NEEDS SOME WORK	KEY AREA FOR ATTEN-TION	DOES NOT APPLY
has been designed or modified so that it is the best for the current situation.	___	___	___	___
17. The intensity of the sales coverage is based on the difficulty of the task and the value of the sales potential. We do not call on all accounts at the same interval but exert measured sales effort.	___	___	___	___

Organizing Other Duties

18. Salesman's regular duties other than sales coverage have already been identified, and he has been given guidelines for carrying them out.	___	___	___	___
19. There is an efficient system that provides operating data to the salesman and he is not burdened with paperwork.	___	___	___	___
20. An organized system for the preparation and approval of territory sales programs is in operation and functioning efficiently.	___	___	___	___

Summary

21. Our total sales coverage plan is effective and will attain our five objectives:

Maintain present sales and profits
Increase business with present customers
Win new accounts in present market segments
Expand into new markets
Regain lost customers.   ___   ___   ___   ___

5 / Setting the Structure of the Sales Force

IMAGINATIVE development of the sales force structure can increase sales volume by a minimum of 10 percent. This chapter will review the steps that can produce more revenue with little added cost. The opportunity to reach and sell more markets, and to be more effective in present sectors, demands more than routine attention to the problem. And yet many sales forces reflect a totally unimaginative approach. Each field representative sells the full line in an exclusive geographic area—he is "Mr. Company." The number of men bears little relation to the potential, and there has been no effort to seek the best combination of selling skills and field deployment.

A market-oriented company needs and deserves the best possible sales force, and the sales manager must systematically complete Step 3 of Phase 2—his sales structure. The major decisions to be made are:

- Who will do the selling?
- What products or services will each salesman or sales organization offer?
- To whom will they be offered, and where?

- Who will perform the nonselling tasks, and how?
- Who will supervise, and how?

Who Will Do the Selling?

There are three alternative solutions for the task of calling on customers and prospects: company employees, individual independent contractors, and marketing organizations. Many companies use all three, tailoring the structure to fit the geography, the market, and the skills required.

Company employees represent the greatest opportunity for supervision and training, but of course also involve the highest fixed expense. If the company is dedicated to the concept of developing men who are "territory managers" rather than the traditional field salesman, a full-time sales force can be extremely productive.

Individual independent contractors include commission salesmen, manufacturers' agents, and brokers. They frequently have an intense knowledge of a specific market segment and have the ability to generate sales volume quickly. The fact that the only expense comes after a sale has been made increases the attractiveness of this kind of selling effort. Lack of control and difficulty in finding out what is going on in the field are negative factors, since the independent contractor thinks of it as "my business" and refuses to take direction or divulge details.

Marketing organizations represent an extension of the individual contractor concept, a pooling of skills by several people. Many manufacturers' agents and brokers offer services that go beyond individual selling effort to include warehousing, servicing, and billing. Special sales organizations that offer temporary support can be of great help in introducing a new product, launching a special campaign, or performing routine merchandising tasks. In the export field, there are marketing organizations so extensive that they exceed in size some of the principals they represent.

What Products or Services Will Be Offered?

The simplest arrangement of the sales force is to have each man sell the full line, but this is not always the best. Unless all the products or services form one clear unit, it is better to divide the assignment into logical components.

Product-type sales forces offer related items. For example, a sales team can be organized to specialize in the sales of appliances. The company may have plants in several locations, and may even have some of its products made by others under contract. The marketing effort is unified because the customer is interested in single source buying, not in dealing with several salesmen from the same company.

Skill-type sales forces can often do the best job when there is need for a high level of technical knowledge. A company making a wide range of fasteners and adhesives could establish a special sales force to work with manufacturers, where expert counsel is needed, and another merchandising-oriented group that would sell similar products in packaged form through retail channels. One company added a complete line of pesticides to its traditional agricultural chemical products. It found that it needed a skill-type sales force and set up a new unit, controlled by a sales manager in the central office but individually assigned to the local sales teams. The presence of these highly trained specialists reassured the full-line salesmen, who developed sales far more quickly than if they had not been given close, proficient sales support.

To Whom, and Where?

The needs of the customer should be reflected in the structure of the sales force. Failure to match the talents of the salesman to the requirements of the account can result in costly but inadequate sales coverage.

Market segment sales forces can be divided by the type of customer or the class of trade. Food brokers exemplify concentrated selling effort to a specific market segment. Chemicals companies often structure a small group of specialists to deal with the giant co-producers that buy in large quantities, and then establish another, larger sales force to sell the company's products directly to users through company-owned distribution points. A very large distributor covering much of West Africa has set up a special organization for the sale and servicing of road-building equipment to contractors and government agencies.

Geographic area sales forces answer the question, "Where will each salesman operate?" If the product line is narrow enough for one man to represent it properly, he may also be able to deal effectively with all the customers and prospects in a given area. With so many alternatives available, however, the creation of a full-line, exclusive-area sales force may be little more than a result of lazy thinking at the management level. Such a simple structure should not be adopted until more imaginative and more effective arrangements have been considered.

Open areas represent the other geographic extreme, where all the sales force is permitted to range over the company's entire marketing area. Not as permissive as it sounds, it sometimes represents the best solution when personal salesmanship is a major factor. Thus one printing company allowed its representatives to call anywhere in the area it could profitably serve. It controlled the customer and prospect list to prevent duplication and eliminate poaching. The big problem with the open area concept is that it is difficult to evaluate the adequacy of total sales coverage, as each man answers only for his own effort.

Exclusive areas for specific market segments. When the sales force has been organized by product or market segment lines, it is often best to assign exclusive geographic areas to each man. A salesman or marketing organization can have the responsibility for all wholesalers in the Southeast or for calling on all electronics manufacturers in New England.

Establishing boundaries. Most sales force structures reflect sensible geographic assignments and the realization that political boundaries do not always coincide with market boundaries. For example, the Delmarva peninsula is treated as a unit, Upper Michigan is linked with Wisconsin, and the two Kansas City markets are considered one entity. One prime concern must be to insure full coverage of the geographic area. The "seams" always suffer, and careful shifting of boundaries, even by small amounts, can improve the territorial structure.

Organizing the Sales Force Structure

Exhibit 11 summarizes many of the options open to a sales manager, and illustrates three ways to organize a sales force. The

Exhibit 11. *Three ways to organize a sales force.*

1. Full-line company salesmen and independent agents (most applicable to the small- and medium-size company).

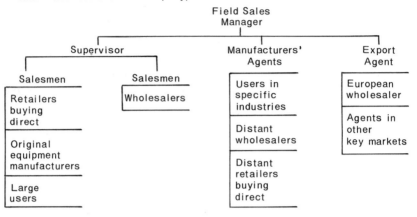

2. A sales force organized by product groups (supply market segments).

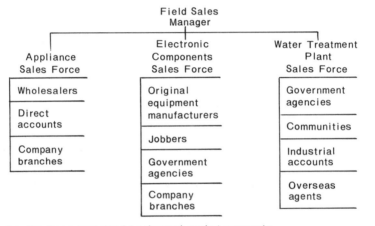

3. A sales force organized by demand market segments.

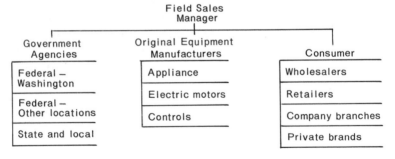

first example shows a simple full-line, exclusive area arrangement, most often applicable to the small- and medium-size company. The second diagram portrays a sales force arranged by product group (supply segments) and the third shows an organization based on demand market segments. The best solution for the individual company often combines elements from all three methods.

Imaginative Sales Structures

Perhaps the best way to demonstrate the value of an imaginative sales structure is to show how one company moved from a limited regional sales coverage to a much more productive one, and yet incurred little expense in relation to the added profit. The product line included pumps, water softeners and conditioners, and powered garden equipment, such as lawn mowers and rotary tillers. The company was controlled by men with production backgrounds. It had superior design and manufacturing, but a completely unimaginative sales force structure, emphasizing full-line company sales-men and wholesale distributors. The sales organization, together with the annual sales volume, is shown in Exhibit 12.

The market-oriented philosophy took hold, and all departments began to search for opportunities to grow. A basic change in strategy called for a new marketing effort involving the sale of components to co-producers and the development of private brand business. Retail sales of water conditioners direct to home and commercial users were profitable, so that component of the sales structure was ex-panded. The policy of selling to well drillers was preventing the company from securing several key wholesale accounts, so it halted its direct sales coverage. Examination of the market for powered garden equipment indicated that the best results could be obtained with two product lines. One emphasized quality and was promoted heavily through one leading retailer in each market; it needed full-time territory managers. The other line emphasized price and was geared for seasonal promotions by discount operations; it was best handled through a regional independent marketing organiza-tion.

Instead of two types of salesmen the company now had five. Territory managers, well trained and highly paid, serviced the major wholesale and retail accounts in three regions and eastern

Canada. An experienced international sales manager was developing excellent volume for proprietary products in several countries and also working on cross-licensing arrangements with a British manufacturer. The former poorly trained commission salesmen had been replaced by highly qualified specialists in the water conditioning field, paid both a salary and a commission. Manufacturers' agents were opening new accounts in the western states and some southern areas, and a marketing organization was securing orders

Exhibit 12. *A manufacturer's original sales force structure and resulting sales volume.*

Market Segment	Sales Force Structure and Annual Volume Produced ($000)		
	Full-time Salaried Salesmen	Commission Salesmen	Total
Pumps			
Wholesalers			
North Central region	$ 300	—	$ 300
Northeast region	450	—	450
Southern region	1,400	—	1,400
Retailers			
Well drillers	1,300	—	1,300
Others	300	—	300
Water softeners and conditioners			
Wholesalers			
North Central region	600	—	600
Users			
Factory sales branch	—	$350	350
Powered garden equipment			
Wholesalers			
North Central region	750	—	750
Retailers			
North Central region	1,100	—	1,100
Total sales volume	$6,200	$350	$6,550

for seasonal merchandise. The sales coverage was far broader, much more relevant to the customer's needs, and produced a greater selling profit.

Not all of the improvement could be attributed to the expanded and improved sales structure; all departments participated in the development of new market segments and the strengthening of existing ones. Sales volume increased 170 percent in five years and the highly seasonal production cycle was perceptibly smoothened. Everyone became interested in finding even more imaginative ways to expand the business. The revised (and far from final) sales structure is illustrated in Exhibit 13.

Who Will Perform the Nonselling Tasks, and How?

When the sales coverage plan was developed (Chapter 4), provision was made for the nonselling tasks that had been assigned to the sales force. Typical duties include warehousing, billing, or performing service functions. In addition, there may be a need to subdivide the selling tasks according to the skill required. A product-type sales force may have day-to-day responsibilities for the demonstration of equipment or the training of new users. In such a case each territory manager might be more efficient if he had one or more technical assistants directly under his control.

Where there is a great deal of administrative work the key structural consideration is to keep both salesmen and supervisors free for the main job—selling. Because the man in the field is "there," he often ends up with work assignments that are far below his skill level and for which he is not temperamentally suited. The frustrated salesman, vainly trying to fathom the intricacies of the company accounting system, is a stereotype. He wants to be with his customers—he should be with his customers—but first he must fill out a complicated monthly inventory report and is thus chained to his desk or to the kitchen table at home.

Who Will Supervise, and How?

One experienced sales executive, fully aware that any selling rule is riddled with exceptions, said, "I would rather have two

Exhibit 13. An improved and expanded sales force structure and resulting sales volume.

Market Segment	Sales Force Structure and Annual Volume Produced ($000)					
	Full-time Territory Managers	Water Treatment Specialists	Application Engineers	Manu- facturers' Agents	Marketing Organi- zations	Total
Pumps						
Co-producers and OEM accounts	—	—	$ 950	—	—	$ 950
Wholesalers						
North Central region	$ 3,100	—	—	—	—	3,100
Northeast region	950	—	—	—	—	950
Southern region	1,800	—	—	$ 300	—	2,100
Western region	—	—	—	400	—	400
Canada	—	—	—	650	—	650
Other export	—	—	—	—	$ 150	150
Private brand accounts	600	—	—	—	—	600
Water softeners and conditioners						
Wholesalers						
North Central region	900	—	—	—	—	900

Northeast region	600	—	—	—	—	600
Southern region	550	—	—	100	—	650
Users						
Company branch, Cincinnati	—	$ 500	—	—	—	500
Company branch, Elgin	—	450	—	—	—	450
Company branch, Columbus	—	350	—	—	—	350
Company branch, Fort Wayne	—	250	—	—	—	250
Valves and controls to co-producers	—	—	350	—	—	350
Powered garden equipment						
Retailers						
North Central region	1,300	—	—	—	800	2,100
Northeast region	650	—	—	—	450	1,100
Southern region	900	—	—	—	450	1,350
Transmissions to co-producers	—	—	300	—	—	300
Total sales volume	$11,350	$1,550	$1,600	$1,450	$1,850	$17,800

good supervisors, each with five salesmen, than have 15 salesmen and only myself to supervise." Supervision of a sales team involves three major duties: (1) direct control of the field effort, (2) training and counseling, (3) reporting to and working with other department managers. Depending on the age and complexity of the business, one of the three duties will usually assume prime importance. The sales manager must make sure that he has the time to handle that key responsibility directly, usually delegating much of the remaining work.

The organization of supervisory duties flows from the basic structure of the sales force. If it is a full-line team, the probable solution is to have regional or branch managers; the key question is whether they should be located at the home office or out in the field. Product-type or market segment sales forces frequently call for two kinds of supervision. The individual salesman may take his orders from a product sales manager at the home office but be attached to a local branch under the day-to-day supervision of the branch manager.

The final area needing resolution is the supervision of nonselling tasks, and the only guideline is to keep the sales supervisors supervising sales. One has only to walk into a sales office, or talk to almost any manager, to know this doctrine is often preached but less and less practiced. The sales manager must build a sales program first and a nonselling program second.

Charting the Structure

Organization charts—you're either for them or against them. In establishing the structure of a sales force, especially for the new or rapidly changing business, an organization chart is essential. A small group of people working in close harmony may be able to get along without a clear definition of relationships, but a sales force? Not hardly. For proof, ask 100 salesmen if they are clear on exactly what their job is, what their relationship is with others in the company, and if their customers understand just what the salesman is supposed to do. The no answers will unfortunately outnumber the yes replies.

The other advantage of an organization chart is that it begins the process of defining the skills and experience needed for each type of job, the first step toward proper recruiting and training. Price tags can be attached, and the sales manager can test the realism of the sales force structure. Unless there are very bright sales opportunities in the near future, it will be hard to justify an $18,000 (plus expenses) man in a distant market, and an agent may be the only solution. From another angle, if an export agent can be found who will work on a commission basis, maybe it's time to stop talking about overseas business and to organize a program that will get some.

Using the examples in Exhibit 11 as a guide, or inventing his own more applicable format, the sales manager should sketch his organization structure. He is almost, but not quite, at the point of saying how many people he needs; certainly the three questions of sales coverage, sales force structure, and the number of people interact constantly. To prepare himself for the final step in Phase 2, a simple sketch of his proposed organization, together with a brief tabulation of the type of people he will need, is essential. For example, the following list covers the key needs of a regional manufacturer.

Company Salesmen (Full-time, with salary and incentive)	University graduate with five years' experience (at least two in sales), able to deal with senior purchasing agents and department heads. Annual average salary and bonus — $18,000.
Field Sales Supervisor	University graduate; successful field salesman; proven leadership, training, and administrative skills. Annual average salary and bonus — $25,000.
Manufacturers' Agents	Experienced with building and construction trade. Commission — 5 percent (more if maintaining stocks of units and parts).
Export Agent	Skills needed have not yet been determined, and cost is unknown. Get answers by December 1.

Setting the structure of the sales force is a challenging assignment. There are so many variations and so many opportunities to expand the existing sales effort that an orderly examination of all the alternatives is essential. Checklist No. 5 can help make sure that each aspect of the sales structure has been carefully evaluated, and that the final outcome is the best combination of skills, selling assignments, and geography.

Checklist No. 5
Setting the Structure of the Sales Force

TOPIC	OK	NEEDS SOME WORK	KEY AREA FOR ATTEN- TION	DOES NOT APPLY
Who Will Do the Selling?				
1. Company-paid salesmen are used when the skills needed are best supplied by full-time territory managers.	___	___	___	___
2. The services of manufacturers' agents are effectively used, particularly for specialized markets and to extend sales coverage.	___	___	___	___
3. The capability of marketing organizations has been analyzed, and we are using them to the best advantage.	___	___	___	___
What Products or Services Will Be Offered?				
4. If we are using a full-line sales force, we have examined other alternatives and found the full-line concept to be best.	___	___	___	___
5. Product-type sales forces are grouped according to the marketing opportunities, and are not based on plant locations, past organization arrangements, or geography.	___	___	___	___

6. We have carefully studied the possibility of organizing skill-type sales ef-

Checklist No. 5
(Continued)

TOPIC	OK	NEEDS SOME WORK	KEY AREA FOR ATTEN- TION	DOES NOT APPLY
fort, and the correct decisions about this specialized technique have been made.	___	___	___	___

To Whom, and Where?

7. The structure of the sales force is based on customer needs. Where special effort for a market segment is needed, we have the correct solution in operation.	___	___	___	___
8. If we use the exclusive area concept, with one salesman handling all products and all accounts, it is because we have proved it is the best structure for us.	___	___	___	___
9. We have considered the possibility of open areas for all or part of our market and have made the correct decision.	___	___	___	___
10. If there are any specialized sales units, their geographic responsibilities have been clearly stated.	___	___	___	___
11. The boundaries of our sales units are the best possible for our market. We have full coverage and there are no boundaries that need changing.	___	___	___	___

Organizing the Sales Force Structure

12. All the options in setting the sales force structure have been examined, and we have an imaginative arrangement that gives us maximum coverage.	___	___	___	___

Who Will Perform the Nonselling Tasks, and How?

13. An efficient structure has been set up to perform the nonselling tasks that

Checklist No. 5
(Continued)

TOPIC	OK	NEEDS SOME WORK	KEY AREA FOR ATTEN- TION	DOES NOT APPLY
have been assigned to the sales force.	___	___	___	___
14. We have also analyzed the possibility of reassigning some of the tasks performed by senior salesmen to other less experienced and costly people.	___	___	___	___
15. The organization of administrative work does not require excessive time from salesmen or supervisors.	___	___	___	___

Who Will Supervise, and How?

16. The supervisory structure represents the best way to provide direction and training for our sales force.	___	___	___	___
17. The sales manager has ample time for his management relations with other departments.	___	___	___	___
18. Supervision of nonselling tasks is effective and does not impair proper supervision of selling effort.	___	___	___	___

Charting the Structure

19. An up-to-date chart clearly defines the structure of our selling, nonselling, and supervisory groups.	___	___	___	___
20. The key skills needed for each major job category have been defined, and cost estimates made.	___	___	___	___
21. The realism and effectiveness of our structure have been tested; it is the best one we can devise. We can now determine the size and location of our sales force.	___	___	___	___

6 / Determining the Size and Location of the Sales Force

THERE are four steps in Phase 2, planning and organizing the field sales effort, and the final one can now be undertaken. Decisions have been made about the principles of customer and prospect coverage, the structure of the sales force, the products each type of salesmen will offer, and the allocation of geographic areas. Now it is time to calculate how many people will be needed and how much the operation will cost. Unfortunately, there is no royal road to the solution of the problem. The answer is contained in what appears to be a simple equation:

$$\text{Size of sales force} = \frac{\text{Total field work to be done}}{\text{Field work one man can do}}$$

The apparent simplicity vanishes because it is not easy to measure the total task or to define what one man can accomplish. Several mathematical formulas have been developed which supposedly calculate exactly the optimum size of the sales force. Most of them, however, are based on rigid concepts of how many calls per year to make on accounts of different value, such as *A, B,* and *C* customers. They assume that all men have similar responsibilities, about the same travel load, put in the same number of hours, and are about equally effective in their work. Any sales manager knows that the converse is true.

The process of determining the size and location of the sales force must therefore be a step-by-step solution, working first with known quantities and then with estimates. Alternatives must be devised and tested and a manning table and trial budget prepared. Finally, after much thought and hard work, a sound final field sales budget can be constructed. The sequence starts with those activities that are definable, or whose size and location have already been determined.

The Measurable Components

In the systematic development of a sales budget, some components can be accurately described and measured. If there has been a decision to use manufacturers' agents in the Pacific Northwest, or to the textile trade, the direct selling cost has probably been fixed as a percentage of sales. It makes no difference whether one marketing organization covers an entire segment or whether a number of agents, one per market, are used. True, there will be some difference when supervision costs are calculated, but the territorial cost is constant.

There may also be clear rules that can be followed in deciding the number and location of people to do nonselling work. Experience may have already shown that three people—a secretary, a billing clerk, and a clerk-typist—are needed at each branch location up to a certain size; there is little point in making endless calculation to prove the need. The decision may already have been made (hopefully on a systematic basis) that only two salesmen will be hired to open the market for a new product or to develop a new geographic area.

The first step, therefore, is to identify those sales activities that have either a fixed cost or a specific number of employees, and tabulate them. Once this is done, attention can be turned to the variables, the greatest of which is the number of salesmen needed to complete the sales coverage. A good way to estimate the size of the sales team is to calculate the selling hours each man can deliver, compare this with the selling hours needed, and thus determine quite accurately the number of salesmen that must be employed.

Calculating Annual Selling Hours per Man

As a rule, and usually an accurate one, a field salesman will have 1,000 hours a year for direct, person-to-person selling. (See Chapter 5 of *Managing a Sales Territory* for a detailed discussion.) Naturally each business has its own individual pattern, but they all can be readily calculated if the following three components are analyzed.

Total selling hours. It is relatively simple to compute the number of hours a salesman spends each year on his major activities: selling, traveling, planning, learning, and nonselling. The annual total of working hours is usually about 2,500, of which around 35 or 40 percent can be classed as selling hours. Many companies have asked their salesmen to make such a calculation. The results are both shocking and encouraging: shocking when everyone realizes how little time is spent performing the central task; encouraging because both salesman and company institute changes to increase the percentage of working time that can be spent with the customer or prospect. In the example that follows, the figure of 1,000 selling hours per man per year will be used.

Developing new accounts. If the structure of the sales force has been efficiently organized, specific percentages can be set for the selling time that each group is to spend developing new accounts. The men breaking into a relatively untapped market segment may spend 50 percent or more of their selling time in such work, while those promoting the company's staple products in established territories may spend as little as 10 percent.

Crises and opportunities. In addition to death and taxes, the sales manager can be certain that there will be unanticipated deviations from his plan, and he must provide the manpower and time to resolve crises and to exploit opportunities. It often helps, in assessing this problem, to think of a business as being either "mechanical" or "electronics," but not in the conventional meaning of the word. A mechanical business is one where the crisis rate is reasonably predictable. Like a mechanical machine, it tends to operate in a relatively constant manner, to require periodic overhaul, and to have trouble about on schedule. Although the sales managers might not agree, grocery and hardware products are mechanical businesses. The electronics business is one where the crisis rate is unpredictable. Sometimes things go smoothly, and sometimes Murphy's law seems to be in force everywhere. (Murphy's law: If anything can go wrong, it will, and at the worst possible time.) In addition to things that have come unstuck, unexpected opportunities spring up. Printing can be an electronics business; so can heavy equipment sales, even though the product is mechanical.

The sales manager needs to state provisions for handling unplanned crises and opportunities. If his business is one in which a salesman can regularly plan his day and work his plan, a 5 percent allowance is ample. If, on the other hand, it is the kind of business where instant attention is needed for recurring crises, he is only fooling himself if he thinks in terms of less than 25 percent allowance.

Allocating selling time. Based on both factual data and realistic estimates, it is now possible to estimate the typical amount of selling time a salesman would have, and how it can be divided among present customers, new business development, and crises and opportunities. Taking the sales force shown in the second diagram in Exhibit 11 as an example, we can give a summary like this:

Type of Salesman	Annual Selling Hours	Developing New Business (%)	Crises and Opportunities (%)	Annual Hours for Existing Accounts
Appliance: major cities	1,200	10	10	960
Appliance: other areas	1,000	10	20	700
Electronics: original equipment mfrs.	1,000	30	10	600
Electronics: other	1,000	10	10	800
Water treatment: U.S.A.	900	50	20	270
Water treatment: international	Varies too much for averaging			

Forecasting Total Selling Hours Needed

Many attempts have been made to calculate the amount of selling time needed to service a group of present customers, and often the result brings only an amused shake of the head from those on the firing lines. The usual trouble is that the area of analysis has become too big and is absorbing many estimates and guesses to produce a final figure that pretends to be an exact measurement. It *is* possible to estimate selling time requirements quite accurately if the group being studied is kept small. In developing the sales coverage plan (Chapter 4), guidelines for the type and amount of sales support to be given each major class of customer were established. The table on the Kansas City Branch is an example of how these judgments can be applied to a branch operation to produce a realistic estimate of the number of selling hours required for effective coverage.

Kansas City Branch

Type of Customer	Number	Annual Selling Hours Planned per Customer	Total Selling Hours Required
Key wholesaler	2	150	300
Wholesaler	6	50	300
Key retailers	22	30	660
Retailers and all other regular accounts	180	15	2,700
Total	210		3,960

Estimating Number of Salesmen Required

The branch manager has already determined that, after providing for the development of new business and for the handling of crises and opportunities, each man will have about 700 selling hours annually to take care of present customers. It seems that the branch will need six salesmen to provide adequate sales coverage, and there is now reasonable documentation to prove the case. Another advantage of this approach, of course, is that it helps to apportion both opportunity and responsibility equally among the salesmen. Excellent team spirit can be counted on when each man is convinced that there are enough salesmen, that he has his fair share of the existing business, and that the coverage expected of him is reasonable.

The technique of calculating the individual salesman's capability and thereby estimating the size of the total task is far from infallible. If a separate analysis is made for each major sales area, and if the buildup of the final figure is carefully done, this method can provide one indicator of optimum size. It can then be tested against other norms, and the final result will be far superior to the unplanned growth, and inadequate coverage, of many sales forces.

Other Measurement Techniques

The Market Potential Method

Particularly when a sales force is being expanded or redeployed, market potential offers a good measurement of the size of the sales force. If the total demand can be determined, and if the company's market share is reasonably consistent, it can allocate salesmen on the basis of proven success in other markets. For example, one chemicals company covered a territory extending about 200 miles in radius from each of its plants; longer shipments involved excessive freight cost and service problems. It found that it could accurately determine the total usage of its kinds of products in each plant's market, and that its successful operations usually got about 15 percent of the potential. A good salesman was fully employed, and profitable, when he was working an area with a total demand of at least $1,000,000 and therefore selling $150,000 to $200,000 annually. As his sales potential reached $2,000,000 he could not cover his area adequately and had to neglect worthwhile prospects or skimp on customer service. If the total potential was much below $1,000,000, he was either underemployed or calling on very small accounts that should not be sold direct.

When the company moved into a new area, or examined the size of the sales force around an existing plant, one test was to plan to have a salesman for each $1,500,000 of total demand. The individual features of each area, such as competition, price, and customer service requirements, could modify the final arrangement, but at least it was founded on the application of principles that the company had proved were sound and profitable.

The Geographic Coverage Method

Some businesses have such a concentration of sales in relatively few geographic markets that the first order of business is to make sure that these key areas are fully staffed. The company first determines how many men it will need in its vital coverage area; the selling hours method already described is frequently used.

The next decision is to resolve the method of working the remaining geography. If the major markets are highly individualistic, the best plan is probably to keep key area salesmen exclusively within each market, and to use additional salesmen or manufacturers' agents to cover secondary and remote markets. On the other hand, when the selling task is the same with a big customer or a small one, it may be better to give each man a two-segment territory, including a portion of the close-in market and a logical portion of the remote areas. In this way it might be possible to attract better salesmen by being more flexible about the individual's headquarters city or town.

Even when a company has tested the size of its sales force against all three norms — selling hours, market potential, and geographic coverage — the analysis is not complete. Additional sales volume may be so profitable that traditional concepts about sales effort and selling expense should be discarded. Incremental sales analysis can provide the answer.

Maximizing Profits Through Incremental Sales

An incremental sale is one that is over and above the planned level. If the annual target is 10,000 units, all fixed and continuing expenses will be prorated against that figure, and when the 10,000th unit is sold, the "burden" has been absorbed. Unit 10,001 theoretically carries a much higher profit, because the only costs remaining to be met are direct and out-of-pocket. Actually, each sale is potentially as profitable as any other, and the concept of incremental sales is based on striving for business that is over and above the level needed for a reasonable return on investment. It means doing more with the same machinery and people.

In determining the size of the sales force it is essential that the cost and value of each salesman be clearly understood. There can be wide differences of opinion on how much business a salesman must produce before he earns his keep. A few examples will illustrate the variations:

Example 1: Conservative Approach

Company net profit after income tax	−7% of sales dollars
Annual cost of a salesman	−$14,000
Sales volume needed to cover cost of salesman $= \dfrac{\$14,000}{0.07}$	$= \$200,000$

Example 2: Factory Cost Approach

Margin between selling price and factory cost of goods sold (before marketing, administrative, and research expenses)	−30%
Annual cost of a salesman	−$14,000
Sales volume needed to cover cost of salesman $= \dfrac{\$14,000}{0.30}$	$= \$47,000$

Example 3: Available Dollars Approach

Margin between selling price and direct, out-of-pocket costs (not counting any fixed or nonvariable expense)	−55%
Annual cost of a salesman	−$14,000
Sales volume needed to cover cost of salesman $= \dfrac{\$14,000}{0.55}$	$= \$26,000$

In the first example, each sale is expected to bear its full cost, whether or not it exceeds planned volume. The factory cost approach in Example 2 provides for all manufacturing expenses, including fixed items that may already have been absorbed when the planned volume is attained. This middle-of-the-road attitude can indicate that the company is not yet fully market oriented, and that "production" and "marketing" are still considered separate and often competing entities. In the final example, and the most controversial one, each sale is theoretically a new one that would not have been obtained unless a new salesman had been employed. Since all the fixed expenses would have gone on in any event, the incremental cost is limited to such items as raw material and direct labor cost. The new salesman, under this concept, very quickly begins to make dollars available for fixed expense or for profit. As soon as he obtains $26,000 in new business he has covered his own cost, plus raw materials and direct factory expense.

Opponents of the available dollars approach make several points. The most obvious is that if all the salesmen rested after reaching the $26,000 level (or even the $47,000 level), the company would go bankrupt under the weight of unabsorbed fixed expense. Others object to the concept of incremental sales because it casts the salesman in the role of profit maker, when in fact all employees in the market-oriented company have contributed. Despite the danger of misinterpretation, the incremental sales approach must be tested. Far too many companies operate with unrealistically high standards of what a "typical salesman" should produce. The question to be asked is, "If we hold everything else constant, and add one salesman, how much *new* business is necessary for him to produce in order to cover his cost as well as the out-of-pocket costs of what he sells?"

Working closely with the accounting department, the sales manager can test several variations of sales force size and expected volume, watching the increase or decrease in probable company profit for each level. He may well find that while four more salesmen can cost $60,000, even average sales results would produce $250,000 in "available dollars," over and above direct costs. Even in a giant company, an additional $190,000 profit merits careful study.

Supervision

The line between supervision and selling is not always clear. A branch manager may have responsibility for the direction of six salesmen and may also handle three accounts personally. Training is usually considered a responsibility of the sales supervisor, but many companies have successfully used experienced salesmen to train new ones. When it comes to actual supervision, experienced manufacturers' agents not only do not need but will not accept the type of direct control appropriate for a group of relatively new salesmen. A rapidly growing company, to take another case, needs far more on-the-job training by skilled supervisors than the static company with few product changes and a stable sales force.

Clearly, therefore, the number of supervisors is a function of the individual sales program. The main problem is that many companies fall short of what should be done. The sales manager can be certain that he will have more crises, more calls on his time, and more decisions to make than he anticipated. If this leads to a sales force that feels isolated and underinformed, the blame lies with the sales manager. He should have programmed and fought for adequate help in the direction, training, and motivation of his team.

Determining the Locations for the Sales Force

Many of the questions about sales force location appear to be solved in advance. The company headquarters is the only place for the sales manager and his administrative and clerical staff, and the regional plants or offices are the best spots for branch managers and supervisors. Saves expense, promotes company spirit, a lot of other good reasons, right? Period. Next subject?

Not in the market-oriented company. The sales force deals with customers and prospects far more than with other employees, and a factory in an industrial zone is seldom the best place for a sales office. The key question about a sales supervisor is not where he should be headquartered, but whether he, and his salesmen, need an office at all.

The location of the sales force ought to reflect some common-sense rules, and usually does. Most salesmen do live near their biggest customers, and in a city or town that makes it possible to cover the entire area with a reasonable amount of travel. After all, it's in the territory manager's own interest to make his working time as productive as possible. Unfortunately, the thorniest problems usually involve the good men. The candidate who is clearly the best for a critical sales assignment lives outside the area, will not or cannot move, and sales boundaries cannot be adjusted without upsetting other good salesmen. What to do? Or else, everybody wants to live in the big city, when the logical arrangement dictates that several men should make their headquarters in smaller towns. It serves no purpose to point out the inefficiencies that result from poor selection of location; they are already well known. The only alternative may be to have less skilled salesmen, and the final solution is arrived at only after weighing many plus and minus factors.

In time most location problems will solve themselves in the market-oriented company. Since it knows its market segments thoroughly, it can clearly identify the best locations for its sales team; many companies, sadly, really don't know where their salesmen should be. Because the market-oriented company offers both a selling opportunity and excellent compensation, it is easier to find men where they are wanted, or to move them. As the company grows it should be able to retain its best men, and through promotion and transfer see that they are headquartered in the best locations. In fact, a company with location troubles is probably viewing the exposed tip of an iceberg of marketing deficiencies. Unable to develop the product line that will win large customers, unwilling to pay for top-flight salesmen, it has gone 180 degrees off course and is trying to increase profits by underspending rather than by selling more.

Preparing a Manning Table

All the calculations and analyses about the size and location of the sales force are now consolidated into a manning table. The table shows the titles for each major position or selling effort, the number of people assigned to each function, and the location of each unit or salesman. It will be even easier to understand if it is accompanied by a map and, where necessary, one or two overlays

Exhibit 14. Manning table for a medium-size company's field sales force.

| Location | Type and Number of Sales Force Members | | |
	Supervisory	Sales	Administrative
Headquarters	Field sales mgr. International sales mgr.		Sales office mgr. 2 Secretaries 1 Billing clerk
Eastern region	Regional sales mgr. (New York) 2 Sales supervisors:	10 Territory mgrs:	Secretary Billing clerk Clerk-typist
	(1) New York	⎧ New York (2) ⎨ Philadelphia ⎪ Washington ⎩ Pittsburgh	
	(2) Boston	⎧ Boston (2) ⎨ Albany ⎪ Hartford ⎩ Buffalo	
Central region	Regional sales mgr. (St. Louis) 3 Sales supervisors:	14 Territory mgrs.:	Secretary Billing clerk Inventory clerk Clerk-typist
	(1) Chicago	⎧ Chicago (2) ⎨ Detroit ⎩ Minneapolis	
	(2) St. Louis	⎧ St. Louis ⎪ Kansas City ⎨ Louisville ⎪ Des Moines ⎩ Denver	
	(3) Dallas	⎧ Houston (2) ⎨ Dallas ⎪ New Orleans ⎩ El Paso	

Exhibit 14. (Continued.)

| | Type and Number of Sales Force Members | | |
Location	Supervisory	Sales	Administrative
Western region	Regional sales mgr. (Los Angeles) Sales supervisor: Los Angeles	4 Territory mgrs.: Los Angeles San Francisco Phoenix San Diego 3 Manufacturers' agents: Portland Seattle Salt Lake City	Secretary Billing clerk Inventory clerk

that portray individual and unit boundaries. Ideally the sales organization map can be compared with those already developed to show present sales and future potential, and its correctness should stand out clearly when measured against the work to be done. Exhibit 14 illustrates one way to organize a manning table.

The Trial Sales Budget

When the manning table is complete, the next step is calculating a trial sales budget and testing it for realism. Exhibit 15 shows an abbreviated sales budget and some of the calculations that can be made to determine if the planned expenditure is consistent with the profitability of the operation.

Completing Phase 2

The step-by-step development of Phase 2—planning and organizing the field sales effort—is now almost complete. Before

Exhibit 15. An abbreviated sales budget.

Expense Category	Sales Unit				
	Head-quarters	Eastern Region	Central Region	Western Region	Total
People					
Supervision					
Salaries	$ 45,000	$ 18,000	$ 20,000	$ 15,000	$ 98,000
Incentive	12,000	4,000	5,000	7,000	28,000
Territory mgrs.					
Salaries	–	135,800	167,600	50,770	354,170
Incentive	–	20,000	26,000	10,500	56,500
Manufacturers' agents					
Commission	–	–	–	80,000	80,000
Subtotal	57,000	177,800	218,600	163,270	616,670
Tools					
Rent or company charge for space	6,000	4,000	5,400	2,800	18,200
Operating equipment and supplies	43,000	11,000	16,000	9,000	79,000
Selling materials, training, and re-cruiting	176,000	18,000	30,000	16,000	240,000
Subtotal	225,000	33,000	51,400	27,800	337,200
Actions					
Automobile expense	5,000	36,000	56,000	18,000	115,000
Travel	28,000	5,000	8,000	7,500⁻	48,500
Trade shows	70,000	14,000	6,000	11,000	101,000
Business entertainment	15,000	8,000	11,000	6,000	40,000
Subtotal	118,000	63,000	81,000	42,500	304,500
Total field sales budget	$400,000	$273,800	$351,000	$233,570	$1,258,370
Budget Analysis					
Compared with esti-mated actual this year —increase or (de-crease)	$ 26,000	$ 16,100	($ 6,900)	$ 41,300	$ 76,500
As a percent of planned sales volume	–	4.4	4.2	8.1	7.0
As a percent of gross profit (sales less cost of goods sold)	–	16.0	10.5	20.3	18.4

settling on the final manning table and field sales budget, it is a good idea to go back once more over all the decisions and changes that have been made to see if any further revisions are needed. Making a plan, sticking to it, and achieving the planned results breeds confidence throughout the organization. Management is happy because it has used each department plan to produce its total plan and is relying on each unit to attain its goals. The sales team is equally pleased when it does what it said it will do. And when budget time rolls around next year, a sound track record increases the chance of getting an even more effective sales program for the future. The checklist that follows includes a review of the topics discussed in this chapter, as well as a section to summarize the major actions needed to make Phase 2 fully effective. The foundation has now been laid for Phase 3 — recruiting, training, and motivating.

Checklist No. 6
Determining the Size and Location of the Sales Force

TOPIC	OK	NEEDS SOME WORK	KEY AREA FOR ATTENTION	DOES NOT APPLY
Sales Force Size				
1. The sales organization chart has been analyzed, and all components that call for either fixed expense or a fixed number of people have been identified and calculated.	____	____	____	____
2. The total selling hours of a salesman have been computed by analyzing his major activities during a year.	____	____	____	____
3. The guidelines for developing new accounts have been established and the percentage of selling time to be used defined.	____	____	____	____
4. Adequate provision has been made for salesmen to handle crises and to ex-				

Checklist No. 6
(Continued)

TOPIC	OK	NEEDS SOME WORK	KEY AREA FOR ATTEN- TION	DOES NOT APPLY
ploit opportunities that are unanticipated.	___	___	___	___
5. The typical division of a salesman's annual selling time among present customers, new accounts, and for unplanned crises and opportunities has been calculated and is realistic.	___	___	___	___
6. Using sales coverage plans already established, we have calculated the selling time needed to cover our various customer groups.	___	___	___	___
7. Both the selling time and the selling need calculations have been combined into an estimate of the number of salesmen required.	___	___	___	___
8. The best size for the sales force has also been estimated by using the market potential method.	___	___	___	___
9. The geographic coverage method has been used to determine sales coverage needs, and results have been compared with the other estimating techniques.	___	___	___	___
10. The value of incremental sales has been developed with the help of the accounting department. We know the breakeven point for the existing sales group and for incremental additions to it.	___	___	___	___
11. Several different sizes of sales forces have been compared and tested for cost and probable profit.	___	___	___	___
12. The final decision about the size of the sales force is based on a careful study of several alternatives.	___	___	___	___

Checklist No. 6
(Continued)

TOPIC	OK	NEEDS SOME WORK	KEY AREA FOR ATTEN-TION	DOES NOT APPLY
Supervision and Administration				
13. The supervisory group has been organized to fit the special needs of our business and can perform all its tasks efficiently.	___	___	___	___
14. The right number and kind of administrative employees are provided for, and nonselling duties will be performed in a superior way.	___	___	___	___
Locations				
15. Every central or unit headquarters location represents the best one for field sales effort.	___	___	___	___
16. The best locations for salesmen and supervisors have been identified, and a deliberate program to put men in those places is in operation.	___	___	___	___
Manning Table				
17. A consolidated manning table has been prepared, showing the type, number, and location of all the major positions in the sales team.	___	___	___	___
18. An up-to-date map shows all boundaries and the disposition of the sales force. It can be compared with other maps that show present sales and total market potential.	___	___	___	___
Sales Budget				
19. A trial sales budget has been developed and tested against pertinent norms and ratios.	___	___	___	___

Checklist No. 6
(Continued)

TOPIC	OK	NEEDS SOME WORK	KEY AREA FOR ATTEN- TION	DOES NOT APPLY
20. The proposed sales organization and budget has been reviewed by company management, marketing management, and other interested departments. Their instructions or comments have been acted on.	___	___	___	___
21. A final manning table and budget have been completed and approved.	___	___	___	___

Review of Phase 2: Planning and Organizing the Sales Effort (Chapters 3 through 6)

All of Phase 2 has now been completed, except for the following items listed under the appropriate step:

Step 1: Defining and Measuring the Sales Task

Step 2: Formulating the Customer and Prospect Coverage Plan

Step 3: Setting the Structure of the Sales Force

Step 4: Determining the Size and Location of the Sales Force

7 / Recruiting the Sales Force

IT would be a blessing if a sales force, once defined and structured, could be bought off the shelf, complete and ready to go. All too often the reverse is true. Having described exactly what he needs in a sales force, the manager realizes that no such thing exists; he must create it by a never-ending cycle of recruiting, training, and motivating. The initial task is to locate and hire men who meet his specifications. Rarely is he able to match exactly the qualities he needs and the skills he finds, so training must close the gap. And as every manager learns over and over, the fact that a man is capable of doing a job does not guarantee that he will do it. Motivation, such as compensation, incentives, and career development, must be provided.

Phase 3 in the development of a complete field sales program transforms a paper organization into a dynamic team of skilled, efficient producers. The first step, recruiting the sales force, is the subject of this chapter. The major components of the staffing function are:

- Defining the needs
- Finding and attracting candidates

- Selecting the best candidates
- Hiring and promoting (and firing)
- Planning for the future

Defining the Needs

Recruiting a sales force involves getting help from others, in or out of the company. Even if he acts as his own personnel department, the sales manager will be advertising, or asking for assistance from customers and friends, and frequently appraising salesmen in related fields or from competitive companies. His search must therefore begin with an accurate description of what he is seeking. The perfect salesman doesn't exist, but that's no reason to stop looking for him—provided he would be recognized.

The "Ideal Man"

The central theme in defining the "ideal man" (or reasonable facsimile thereof) is to think in terms of results, or consequences, rather than in terms of skills or experience. The effective salesman is one who can make certain things happen; proper background increases his chances of success, but is only one factor. The emphasis must be on men who can produce, not merely those who have an inventory of business talents. Add to this the desirable personal characteristics the salesman should have, and the result is a definition of the ideal man, for one type of job in one company.

Field salesmen. If the search is aimed at finding salesmen who are results oriented, the successful candidates will also be men who think and act like territory managers, not merely territory workers. They will have the independence, the self-reliance, and the willingness to work hard that are the marks of a successful manager. A salesman with a managerial attitude believes that he is in charge of a specific phase of his company's operation and that he is responsible for directing it to the achievement of its objectives. The territory worker, on the other hand, waits to be told what to do, accepts little responsibility, and resents training and counseling as an implied criticism.

In addition to this management outlook, the ideal salesman will possess other qualities dictated by the market segments in which he works. A printing company found that its successful men had a strong technical background and that lack of this trait meant almost certain failure. Conversely, the best salesmen for a grocery products manufacturer may not know how the products are made, since that technical information is of no interest to the buyer who is concerned with merchandising and distribution. The swing in qualities, depending on the type of sales results to be produced, is illustrated in the chart that follows.

	Capital Goods	Intangibles	Durable and Industrial	Mass Market
Salesman's responsibility for the steps of a sale	High	High	Medium	Low
Technical knowledge	High	High	Medium	Low
Willingness to work exact schedule and program	Low	Low	Medium	High
Entrepreneurship (ability to generate own program)	High	High	Medium	Low

Establishing a Sales Profile

Having talked to customers, and studied the reasons for success and failure of his competitors, the sales manager will usually find that the ideal salesman is one who understands the customer's business, has a good technical background in *his customer's skill areas*, and has complete knowledge of his own company's selling points and capabilities. Notice the emphasis on the customer's skill areas. Selling to an auto parts wholesaler may not call for much knowledge of how the parts are made, but it calls for expert knowledge of how a wholesale business operates.

The results to be produced and the ingredients for success in field selling should be combined in a sales profile that can be used to define duties, screen candidates, determine training needs, and ultimately evaluate performance. Exhibit 16 shows a brief

Exhibit 16. A territory manager's position guide.

Position: Territory Manager, Lawn and Garden Products

Responsibility

To develop a merchandising program based on distribution through wholesalers, and then manage the territory to achieve the volume and selling profit goals.

Results Expected

1. A comprehensive wholesale network provides coverage of all major market segments, and the territory goals are being attained.
2. A business development plan identifies key wholesale and retail prospects and is gaining new accounts.
3. A continuing series of consumer meetings, dealer training programs, and cooperative advertising campaigns is building demand for our products at all distribution levels.
4. Wholesalers' inventories and key retailers' stocks are correctly reported, and accurate forecasts of demand are made monthly.
5. Requests for assistance or complaints from users and from the trade are efficiently handled.

Duties and Activities

1. Develop individual annual programs for each wholesale account, assisting the customer in selling retailers and users and helping him to attain maximum sales and profits from the distribution of our products.
2. Work with wholesalers' salesmen in the field, imparting product and technical knowledge to them and aiding them in increasing business with retailers and major users.
3. Assist golf course superintendents and other managers of large turf areas in developing sound annual programs built around our products.
4. Actively seek speaking engagements with garden clubs and professional groups such as nurserymen and superintendents.
5. Secure advance commitments from wholesalers and key retailers, including product orders, advertising tie-ins, and floor displays.
6. Maintain close contact with our credit manager, and assist in keeping outstandings within approved limits and in securing prompt payment for shipments.

Exhibit 16. (Continued)

7. Arrange for monthly inventory reports from wholesalers, either taking them personally or securing reliable cooperation.
8. Furnish an accurate forecast of high and low limits of demand, by product, monthly during the spring and fall seasons.
9. Be informed about market factors in the territory, including all wholesalers, their distribution and pricing policies, and lines carried. Know key retailers and the decision makers in each major account. Maintain good relations with experiment and extension services.
10. Organize and carry out weekly work plans that are consistent with company sales coverage guidelines.

Education, Experience, and Personal Qualities
1. A high school diploma is required, and college-level studies in agriculture or business administration are an asset. A college degree, with a major in agronomy or marketing, is ideal.
2. Must know or acquire knowledge of lawn and garden chemicals and their properties and be able to recommend application programs. Experience working for a wholesaler, dealer, or manufacturer in the garden supply or hardware field is an asset.
3. Previous sales responsibility, preferably involving management of his own sales territory, is very desirable.
4. Experience in securing distributor and dealer support for a manufacturer's merchandising program is a plus.
5. Must have or be able to develop skill in oral communication. An outgoing personality and the ability to address groups of 25 to 100 people are important. Skill in writing is not critical.
6. Golf and gardening are excellent hobbies and will make it easier to develop close relations with customers and users.

Logical Sources and Logical Promotion Route
1. The best source has been those men with experience selling turf, garden, or agricultural equipment or materials. Our company technical service units provide good candidates. Salesmen with backgrounds in intangibles and mass market products have not been among our most successful territory managers.
2. Logical promotion is to sales supervisor, regional service manager, or assistant service manager, or to a marketing or development assignment in company headquarters.

results-oriented position guide for a territory manager. From time to time this guide will be revised to incorporate the traits of those who succeeded in the job. Chapter 12 will outline a program for analyzing the results obtained by the sales force, and will also show how to translate these appraisals into an even more effective hiring program.

Supervisors. The ideal supervisor was really defined when the structure of the sales force was established. If the company recruits men recently out of school or military service, it can probably expect high turnover. The key supervisory needs include training, close supervision, and ability to redeploy the sales force to cover temporarily vacant areas. The profile is far different from that of a man supervising a group of experienced and successful manufacturers' agents. He will be expected to make the agent feel that he has a permanent connection with a responsible principal, and that he should therefore invest his time heavily in developing sales. The words "training" and "supervision" will never be used, although the responsibilities remain.

Accurate definition of supervisory needs by developing position guides has another and longer-term benefit. It is easier to promote from within and to have trained candidates on the sales force so that the best man, rather than the only man, can be promoted.

Administrative and nonselling employees. It is sometimes said that position guides are needed for managers and even salesmen but not for secretaries, clerks, and warehousemen. The truth is that they are just as badly needed, although the descriptive detail can be compressed. In any company, and especially in a growing one, each employee is entitled to ask, "What am I expected to do?" and "What constitutes doing a good job?" Brief guides help to make sure that all the results expected are attained and that the whole sales team works together harmoniously. Nothing more complicated than a 3″ × 5″ card is needed to list for each person his or her responsibility, the results to be achieved, and the key duties to be performed.

Building communication bridges. The development of a position guide or job profile should never be a one-man job. The ideal solution is to have each employee contribute his ideas about what he does, how he goes about it, and what he is trying to accomplish. Efficiency on the job will usually increase as each person finds out that he is not always being ordered about, but rather that he can help decide ways and means. At the same time, the boss cannot abdicate his resposibility by automatically approving whatever is brought to him. The goal is mutual agreement on responsibilities and duties. When, at a later stage, this agreement is supplemented by individual, jointly developed standards of performance, the productivity level will be high indeed.

Manpower Needs

The scope of the recruiting program needs to be tied to the near-term manpower needs. If too few candidates are attracted, the company will have to settle for a sales staff of marginal quality. In addition, it will be difficult to upgrade the sales force by separating the poorest performers, since no better replacements will be available. On the other hand, too many candidates can cause problems, mostly with the agencies, schools, and customers who referred the applicant to the sales manager. These recruiters will soon stop looking for men when the recurring answer is, "No openings now."

In establishing his recruiting drive, the sales manager must include a realistic allowance for the time needed to find and train a new man; six months is not too high a figure to use initially. Having surveyed his present force and analyzed his expansion needs, he can prepare a simple table, such as the accompanying one, that focuses attention on the recruiting goal.

Sales Force Needs — Next Calendar Year	
Additions	*Replacements*
Regional manager—West Coast	1 Supervisor (retiring)
Territory managers—6	5 to 7 Territory managers
Manufacturers' agents	(3 urgent)
Kansas City	
Mexico	

Definition of manpower needs is essential. Without a continuing recruiting effort, the company will find that it has lost its market orientation at a critical point. It may have done everything else well, but if it has too little sales effort, either in quantity or quality, it will not attain its objectives.

Finding and Attracting Candidates

The basic decision in developing the sales team is whether to buy or build, and the answer usually is to build. Buying a sales force by enticing men away from competitors may have significant short-term advantages in the sales volume produced. This can be more than offset by the long-term problems of controlling the performance and directing the efforts of men who feel that, having been acknowledged as experts, they are above being told what to do and how to do it.

The goal of a candidate development program is to make sure that those who could join the sales force are aware of the opportunity and think favorably of it. Advertisements and placement bureaus spread the word widely, but sometimes the competition for attention drowns the message — so many firms are advertising and searching. A more individual approach is to enlist the help of customers and suppliers, technical associations, and schools and scholars who can work largely on a man-to-man basis in developing interest. Even though he has decided to build rather than to buy his sales force, the sales manager is on the alert for men who are dissatisfied or stymied and wish to leave a competitor. And, of course, to make sure that he does not neglect his closest opportunity, he regularly reviews his fellow employees, looking for candidates for the sales force and for promotable men already on his team.

Advertising

Probably the most commonly used, and most often abused, way to search for candidates is by advertising. The same test that was applied in defining the type of man needed should be applied to the efforts to find him, and the key question is, "What result is expected from our advertising?" The man being sought is busy, self-confident, and security conscious. The advertisement must therefore gain his attention, treat him as an equal, and protect his identity. Following a few tested principles can increase both the number and quality of the replies to advertisements.

Schedule multiple insertions. Before taking action, a job candidate goes through the standard pattern of the steps of a purchase. He must be aware of the employment opportunity. It must be portrayed in a manner that arouses his interest. He will then compare the benefits he could gain from replying against the dangers of disclosing his name, and he must make a positive decision. Only then will he open communications with the employer. One advertisement, run one time, will attract some response, but three or more insertions are probably needed. Only this cumulative message will find the best prospects and move them through those steps they must take before picking up phone or pen.

Emphasize buying motives. The ad should spell out the company's primary buying motive, the one central result that the salesman will be expected to accomplish. If it cannot, it's too early to start the hiring process, because the company doesn't know what it's looking for and more work is needed in defining the sales task. By emphasizing its buying motive, the company automatically screens out many replies from those who lack the skills and experience needed; it will get a much more qualified group of candidates.

Make it easy to reply. The top-flight prospect for a sales force may already be a top-flight salesman in his present position. He knows that he is a success, and he wants to keep his identity confidential. Writing a letter of application may appear to him to be taking a submissive position, and he expects to be treated at least as an equal. Besides, he may need more information about the opportunity before deciding if he is seriously interested.

Many companies will run a blind ad calling for a written reply as a screen against unqualified applicants. Such ads hamper the search for field salesmen, who are essentially oral communicators, dedicated to exchanging information rather than to engaging in fencing matches. A telephone number and the name of a person to ask for make it easy for the good man to test the market, and easy for the company to attract the most (including some poor) replies. Even though it appears to be time consuming, the best approach is to have the phone calls come directly to the man who will do the hiring. He knows what he wants, is skilled at interviewing, and can answer questions decisively and correctly.

Don't screen too closely. Whatever the recruiting techniques, it pays to see a lot of candidates rather than a few. One company told applicants that it planned an initial ten-minute meeting, with other conferences to follow if there was mutual interest. The interview was deliberately designed to see how the candidate made use of limited time to tell his story — exactly the condition he would face every day in the territory. Many of the candidates who were ultimately hired might never have been seen if the initial replies had been screened too closely. The company learned that its best men were not necessarily skilled at letter writing or telephone selling, but they were masters of the personal conference.

Writing the Advertisement

An advertisement that will attract the best candidates is not easy to write, but the principles already mentioned will help. Even after it is written, every ad can be criticized. Those on page 129 are only examples of what to say and what not to say. They do illustrate two different approaches to the same task, that is, getting replies from the men the company needs on its sales force. The first one incorporates the ideas discussed in this chapter; the second is, unfortunately, typical of too many help wanted ads.

Selecting the Best Candidates

Sales managers ought to do a good job of screening candidates and picking the best one. A systematic selection process should, like any buying program, move through the steps of identification, checking, and testing. Having dealt with buyers and purchasing agents for years, a sales executive knows the logical sequence, but does he always use it? The turnover in sales forces raises the question of how effectively new salesmen are chosen. Careful attention to the initial interview, followed by thorough evaluation of supporting information, can increase the probability of success.

TERRITORY MANAGER
OEM AND DISTRIBUTOR DEVELOPMENT
VALVES AND CONTROLS

The Fluidtrol Corporation needs a Territory Manager who can get OEM accounts to specify and buy its valves and controls and who can establish and develop stocking distributors. To deal successfully with customers, our salesman should have an engineering degree, knowledge of hydraulics, and practical experience in selling or working with metering devices.

We do our best to promote from within, and this opening results from the advancement of the present territory manager. We seek a man who is building a career in sales and marketing. Salary, commission on sales, company car, and outstanding benefit programs.

If you want the opportunity to manage your own sales territory, call James Reid at 946-2384, and discuss your experience and qualifications, or ask for more information about this position.

Your response is completely confidential, and no inquiries will be made without your prior approval.

VALVES AND CONTROLS
SALES REPRESENTATIVE

We need an experienced salesman to work a three-state area selling valves and controls. Only those with engineering background should apply. Interviews will be held in Chicago the week of August 24. Write, giving your experience and salary requirements, to Box 683.

Interviewing

Most people approach an interview from the standpoint "What do I want to find out?" That is not the way to interview a prospective salesman. The key question is, "What do I want the candidate to do during the interview?" The goal of the meeting is not to help the interviewer form an opinion. The primary goal is to discover how the salesman thinks, acts, and reacts.

Sometimes the trouble starts with the original employment form. It may be the standard company document, designed to cover all jobs and candidates—managerial, marketing, production, and clerical. Replacing the all-purpose form with one that is tailored to the company's sales needs means getting better information and saving time during the interview. It points out areas to be probed such as sales successes or apparent failures. It makes the prospective employee feel that he is being considered for a specialized team of experts.

During the interview, some of the key indicators to be watched are:

• *Interest.* How much has he tried to find out about us? Does he see us as a prospective customer; has he tried to find out our buying motives and objections?

• *Preparation.* What has he done to increase his effectiveness during the interview? Has he brought any proof that he can do a good job for us?

• *Skill.* We know what our customers are like; what would they think of this man? Would they respect him and turn to him for counsel? Would they like to be with him?

• *Reactions.* How does he handle himself? If put under stress, will he remain composed? If purposely diverted from what he was saying, can he regain control? What would his reactions probably be in difficult situations with our customers and prospects?

• *Desire.* Does he want the job, and has he made it clear that he does? Has he expressed confidence in his ability?

The final outcome, of course, is that the interviewer does form an opinion. But it is an opinion of *what actions the other person took.*

Multiple or single interviews? From the questions listed above it is clear that any interviewer must know a great deal about the sales situation to make intelligent judgments about a candidate for the sales force. It is an argument against the tendency to send the prospective employee on a round of visits, spending 15 to 30 minutes apiece with a half-dozen managers from personnel, production, credit, and research. The only reason for doing so is to get their opinion, and most of the time that opinion is not of great value for the job that is open. They simply do not know the details of territory management and therefore cannot evaluate the prospect in the right terms.

A better course is to restrict the contact with the candidate to one or two people who know the job requirements in detail and to have them see the applicant several times. The man being sought will be dealing with his customers for months and years, and his ability to wear well and to appear to advantage at all times is critical. Far better to let a few people form an in-depth impression than to get flash reactions from a large group.

Checking Credentials

When the search has been narrowed to one or a few candidates, it is time to make careful checks—both preventive and positive. The preventive check makes sure that those being considered have not supplied false or misleading information; it is best done by people or organizations skilled in verifying data. Positive checking, on the other hand, seeks to confirm ability and accomplishment and to assist in the comparative ranking of several candidates. It should be done by the man who will make the hiring decision.

Using the position guide he has already drawn up, the employer should talk to the candidate's references and former employers directly. Usually he will find them flattered by the personal touch and willing to talk freely. This approach is far more effective than the stereotyped letter stating that so-and-so has been listed as a reference and asking for confirmation of employment dates or a brief appraisal of the prospect. The market-oriented company takes a much more dynamic attitude. Consider what reaction this telephone call would bring:

"I'm _____, and I am considering employing _____ as a sales territory manager, reporting to me. His duties would be _____, _____, _____, _____; and we would expect him to produce these results: _____, _____, _____. If he does join us, I want him to make as much progress as possible. Can you help me by answering these questions:

1. Would he do a good job for us, and why do you say so?
2. What would you expect to be his strong points?
3. Where do you think he would need help?
4. Is there anything else I should know to help me in making the decision about hiring _____?"

When the person doing the checking has an obvious interest (as a boss would have), when he talks in specific terms, and when his goal is to help his new men to be good in their jobs, he can expect more than the vague generalities that so often form the reply to a written or routine telephone reference check.

Testing

When the time for decision draws near, the right kind of testing can produce worthwhile information about the candidates. Testing should be used only as a check on judgment. A good rule to follow is that if a test result is the deciding factor in the employer's decision, then the hiring process has gone astray. Outside opinions are a valuable component of any systematic analysis, but the final selection should be an individual judgment by the direct supervisor. Else how can he be held responsible for making the new man a profitable salesman?

Testing falls into two broad categories. Aptitude and psychological tests attempt to compare the candidate with a set of norms and to indicate the level of intelligence, the personality traits, and the probable work habits. They have their place, and each sales manager must define "their place." The other form of testing is field testing, exposing the man to the job and the job to the man.

If at all possible the prospective salesman should get an opportunity to evaluate the key factors of the vacant position. Perhaps he already sells the same kind of products and needs a factory visit where he can obtain involved technical data to convince him that he can sell effectively for a new employer. He may be merchandising oriented and want to know about promotion plans or the state of distribution in the territory he will take over. The more chance he has to change unknown factors into known ones, the deeper will be his personal commitment as he begins the job. Far too many salesmen step into a territory without really knowing what to expect, and most of the time they are disillusioned.

Field testing also gives the company a chance to study this potential salesman closely. Did the factory confirm his technical skill? Is the advertising manager eager to have this man handle local tie-ins, or did he just shrug his shoulders? It's asking a lot to expect people to evaluate a man after a brief encounter, *except* when they are asked about areas in which they are expert.

Some sales managers think that a few days of field exposure and a few hundred dollars expense is too much time and money to devote to the hiring of one salesman. Compared with the ten or fifteen thousand dollars lost when a new man does not work out, it's great insurance at low cost—self-liquidating, too, because the new man will make faster progress in winning sales and earning profits.

Staffing from Within the Company

Armed forces frequently use the cadre system to staff newly formed units. An artillery battery, for example, will be called on to furnish the 15 or 20 key men around whom another artillery battery could be built. Commanders at one time found this a convenient way to ship out some of their less successful noncoms, but headquarters soon got wise. A revised order told them to form two cadres, and at the last moment they would be told which group would stay and which would go to the new assignment. They understandably began to balance strengths and weaknesses, not knowing which cadre would remain. The moral is that staffing from within can be effective, provided the same appraisal techniques are employed as would be used for a prospective new employee. The sales force wants successful performers, not castoffs.

The key advantages of this staffing method are the time saved and the reduction of uncertainty. Sometimes the man can step into his new assignment with little need for special training. His performance has already been analyzed and he comes as a known quantity; it should be easier to improve his selling skills than it would be with a totally new employee. The move from desk or technical work to field selling may be a big jump, but it can be a planned one, producing spectacular success.

Even more rewarding is when a salesman can be promoted to supervisor. First, it documents the realism of the company's compensation and career development program; good men do stay, and they do get promoted, and the rest of the sale force notices. Second, it offers the same advantages of saving time and reducing uncertainties already mentioned in transferring men to the sales force. Finally, it smooths the training task. Hiring a manager from outside may mean hiring an expert, at least in his view. A promotion within the company makes the development of an individualized training program a logical and normal step.

Hiring and Promoting (and Firing)

Hiring

The best available candidate has been identified, and it may seem that the logical thing to do is to hire him before he gets away. Not yet. Particularly with a new salesman, the moment of hiring offers many opportunities to establish a relationship that will endure for years. Adding a man to the sales team must be a two-person exercise; the company must want the man, but just as strongly the man must want the job. There must be agreement on the relationship between the salesman and his immediate superior, particularly in these days of complicated sales force arrangements and often confusing lines of authority. And there must be a definition of the results expected and the steps to be taken to improve existing skills. Failure to nail down these points means trouble later. Several guidelines point the way toward the right way to hire a new salesman.

Hire only enthusiastic men who want the job. The need for individual commitment is the major reason for building, rather than buying, a sales organization. By going through a careful selection process, it is possible to find men who want the job because of the challenge and the rewards they see, who are committed to being a success, and who recognize that the right kind of training helps them achieve their goals. The salesman who is purchased from a competitive force, or who seems indifferent about joining the team, may feel that he knows all about the job. He will probably accept little counsel (or none if it's called training) and he may already have decided that if things don't work out, it certainly couldn't be his fault.

Have the immediate superior make the hiring decision. Only the frequent violation of this rule makes it necessary to emphasize it. If there is to be leadership, control, and accountability for results, there must be a man-to-man relationship. The new salesman must perceive clearly that his immediate supervisor made the decision to hire him, that he can probably help him get promoted, and doubtless can fire him. Even though the top brass may be nodding approvingly offstage, and even though the personnel office handled many of the details, the new man's boss must make the offer of employment and receive the acceptance and commitment.

Establish a training program immediately. The time to begin improving a man's performance is the moment he begins work; to delay means that training will appear to be a correction of mistakes or of shortcomings that have been found. Delay also induces reluctance on the salesman's part; he may be afraid to confess that he does not know all he should or could about his job. If the goal on on the first day of employment (or before, if possible) is to provide the salesman with the knowledge and talents needed to assure superior performance, training becomes a joint venture. Chapter 8 discusses tested ways to establish individual programs.

Set an initial task and a reward. Salesmen thrive on success, particularly visible success. When the new man is employed, some specific task should be set that can be accomplished soon. It may be to get the first order from a prospect already receiving attention, or to bring back a lost customer, or to secure merchandising cooperation from a group of accounts. When the task is completed, reward the man (and his family). Do something to make him glad that he joined, and let him be seen by others, inside and outside the company, as doing well in his new position.

If a planned hiring program is followed, the man will not merely "start" his job. He will confidently take over his assignment, determined to do the best he can and convinced that he will get all the help possible as he strives to attain his goals.

Promoting

Choosing the best man for promotion calls for evaluation and selection, and the steps listed for hiring are just as applicable, from the initial drawing of the job profile or position guide through the search, comparison, and startup phases. Fortunately, promotions tend to work out well, probably because there are more known quantities being dealt with than in the initial hiring process. The truism still holds that a lot of good salesmen are promoted to sales manager and never should be, but that is usually because the company lacks the kind of parallel development program discussed in Chapter 9.

The realistic sales manager knows that moving up to the supervisory ranks can often increase rather than lessen a man's tensions. He may have even more doubts about his ability to succeed, and yet be totally unable to admit that he needs training. Even though he now directs others and praises or criticizes them, he could have an even greater need for recognition and for the approval of his associates. Finally, he may be unsure of his personal relationships, of exactly who is his boss and of what authority others may have over him and his team. Promotion should be a time for the same searching review of responsibilities, skills, and needs as took place on the day the new supervisor first joined the company as its newest salesman.

Firing (Including Reassigning)

Along with the privilege of hiring people comes the duty of separating or reassigning those who have not succeeded in their assignments. By whatever name it is called, it means failure — somewhere. The enlightened approach is to take a no-fault attitude except where there has been impropriety. The important goal is to profit from the mistake, to make a better use of the individual's talents and the company's funds. When should a man be relieved or changed? While it's hard to set fast rules, it seems only right that no one can in fairness be held accountable for poor performance unless these five points can be documented:

1. He knew what he was expected to do. His duties were explained to him in writing and thoroughly discussed.
2. He knew what constituted doing a good job. Through a standard of performance, quota, or task, he was told what results were expected from him, and he committed himself to achieve them.
3. He knew that his performance was unsatisfactory. In a person-to-person interview, the areas in which he was not doing a good job were pointed out to him, and he was given every opportunity to present his views.
4. He knew what improvements were expected and when. A specific program to attain clear objectives was established, including target dates.
5. He failed to attain a satisfactory level of performance by the target date.

Then, and only then, can failure be admitted on both sides. To discharge or transfer a man without completing these five steps is a waste of talent, a waste of company assets, and an unfair act to someone who may have been doing what he thought was a good job. Without this five-step procedure the only failure is the boss.

Planning for the Future

Even a company that budgets ample time and money to find the best man for a vacant position will sometimes fail to prepare adequately for the future. There are so many pressing problems for today that it's hard to worry about a distant cloud; besides, it may go away. This attitude can come from the same marketing group that would be horrified if production were to say the same about its problems. Everybody knows that if you want 10,000 units a month next year, and improved ones at that, you must plan for them today.

Planning the future recruiting program is not really a burdensome task if it is divided into its logical components of demand, recruiting techniques, and improved performance.

Demand. Future needs can be cataloged, and accurate projections of planned growth can be made in the market-oriented company. The whole purpose of the corporate profit plan is to provide guidance for the tactical commanders, such as the field sales manager. Setting up a tentative manning table for three years ahead is far better than a recurring series of crash expansions, followed by the separations that inevitably follow hasty selection and inadequate training.

As a start, take the manning table now in use. Allow for all the men who will retire in three years' time (often not very much of a problem with a small sales force). Face up to the realities of the turnover rate, and estimate the number of replacements needed. The total equals the number of men needed to maintain the status quo three years from now. With the missions and strategies of the company defined, expansion plans for the sales force can be better than educated guesses; they can be realistic projections. When all the components are added, the demand over the next three years is clear. The next question is how to fill it.

Recruiting techniques. Just as the company decided whether to buy or to build its sales force, it must decide how it will bring in the men of the future. Under the investment philosophy, one company encourages branch managers to keep a sales trainee at all times by transferring part of the cost from the local profit-and-loss account to the central office. Another company is equally convinced that it cannot hold the men it wants in a trainee role, and that those willing to become trainees are not really capable of independently managing a sales territory. It has increased its compensation level, lets somebody else do the initial training, and hires only experienced, successful salesmen. Whatever the merits of either plan, each company has taken a position and backed it with money. It has a program.

Improved performance. Later on in this book the methods of analyzing sales force performance will be discussed. As part of that program, periodic improvement of recruiting criteria is essential. The company will be able to determine the relative success of its salesmen, but what does this mean in the search for new men? Are the best men modifying the way they do their job? If so, the position guide must be revised, which means a change in the hiring specifications. How were the leading salesmen brought into the company, and where did the unsuccessful ones come from? Perhaps the educational standards or the prior experience requirements need adjustment. If the best salesmen started in the shop or in the laboratory, should that particular program be expanded? Why is the sales force as good as it is, and what lessons can be drawn that will improve the recruiting and selection process?

Summary

The sales manager has now considered all the responsibilities and the decision areas that make up Step 1 of Phase 3. The checklist that follows will help him collect his thoughts and evaluate his recruiting, selection, and hiring program. To be short of field sales talent often indicates a lack of realism on management's part. The men who can do the job are out there, but the company must know what it wants, how to find it, and be prepared to pay the price.

Checklist No. 7
Recruiting the Sales Force

TOPIC	OK	NEEDS SOME WORK	KEY AREA FOR ATTEN-TION	DOES NOT APPLY
Defining the Needs				
1. Position guides or sales profiles have been prepared for each type of salesman, and they emphasize the need for results-oriented territory managers not for territory workers.	___	___	___	___
2. Supervisory needs have also been defined by the preparation of position guides.	___	___	___	___
3. We have also developed brief guides for administrative and nonselling positions, so that each person knows what he or she is expected to do.	___	___	___	___
4. All the above have been made up				

Checklist No. 7
(Continued)

TOPIC	OK	NEEDS SOME WORK	KEY AREA FOR ATTEN-TION	DOES NOT APPLY
with the active participation of those who will do the job. They are joint efforts and there is mutual agreement on responsibilities and duties.	____	____	____	____
5. Our near-term manpower needs have been defined; we know how many additions and replacements will be needed in the next year.	____	____	____	____

Finding and Attracting Candidates

6. We have an organized program for finding candidates both inside and outside the company.	____	____	____	____
7. Our advertising of vacancies is drawing many replies from the type of men we try to attract.	____	____	____	____
8. Our customers, suppliers, and other influence groups know of our needs, and help us by sending candidates to us.	____	____	____	____

Selecting the Best Candidates

9. Our interviewing program helps identify the best candidates. Only those company employees who can contribute to the hiring decision participate, and we have a planned way to form the correct in-depth impression of each man interviewed.	____	____	____	____
10. Every prospective employee is given a thorough preventive check and all information supplied by him is verified.	____	____	____	____

Checklist No. 7
(Continued)

TOPIC	OK	NEEDS SOME WORK	KEY AREA FOR ATTEN-TION	DOES NOT APPLY
11. Positive checking with previous employers is done by the person who will make the hiring decision, and we learn a lot about the candidate.	——	——	——	——
12. We use aptitude and psychological testing programs, but only as a check on judgment. They give us helpful guidance and we have found that the test results are usually borne out in performance.	——	——	——	——
13. Whenever possible, we schedule a few days of field testing, so that we and the candidate can better appraise the chances of doing a good job.	——	——	——	——
14. We regularly review our own employees for all vacancies, and we identify those who can handle new or greater responsibilities, or can be trained to do so.	——	——	——	——

Hiring and Promoting (and Firing)

TOPIC	OK	NEEDS SOME WORK	KEY AREA FOR ATTEN-TION	DOES NOT APPLY
15. When we hire a new employee, the immediate superior makes the hiring decision, and the line of command and direction is completely clear.	——	——	——	——
16. An individual training program is developed immediately with the participation of the new man.	——	——	——	——
17. We deliberately take action to make the new man be seen as doing well in his work, and he knows how we feel.	——	——	——	——

18. When we promote an employee, he helps design his own training program

Checklist No. 7
(Continued)

TOPIC	OK	NEEDS SOME WORK	KEY AREA FOR ATTEN- TION	DOES NOT APPLY
and we take steps to make him feel confident in his new assignment.	___	___	___	___
19. If a person is to be fired or reassigned, it is only after we make sure that he knew what he was expected to do, that we agreed with him on a program for improvement, and that he failed to attain the performance level set for him.	___	___	___	___

Planning for the Future

20. We are preparing adequately for the future. A manning table showing our coming needs has been prepared, based on the company profit plan.	___	___	___	___
21. We have tested our recruiting techniques and they are the best ones we can devise.	___	___	___	___
22. We periodically review our recruiting techniques in the light of actual salesmen's results, and make further improvements in our methods and criteria.	___	___	___	___

8 / Developing Skills

TELL a salesman that he's going to be trained and he bristles. Training implies remedying deficiencies or getting rid of bad habits, and he will rarely (except to himself) admit to either. Titles such as "orientation courses," "product information meetings," "workshops," "seminars," and on and on, have been devised to make the activity more palatable. Yet, no universal word has been found that describes the function as accurately as "training," and that is the one we shall use, knowing that it may have to go public under another label.

Successful sales training is based on mutual contribution of knowledge. The trainer can impart skills, but the one being trained often knows more about the individual application of those skills. Thus the experienced salesman joining the company will have to learn the product features, but he knows how to present them to customers and prospects. The technical employee being transferred to sales needs training in salesmanship, in how to use his expert product knowledge. In the market-oriented company, the training emphasis is not so much on selling as on helping people buy. The goal is to develop a man who can assist the customer in moving through the steps of a purchase—attention, interest, comparison, conviction, and action. The salesman must be skilled in the eyes of the customer. He does not need to know how the product works, except to be able to show how it fills the buyer's needs. Instead of being trained in company procedures, he must be trained in how to use those procedures to insure fast customer service. Results-oriented training concentrates on developing the service capability of the territory manager.

Step 2 in Phase 3 of the development of a complete field sales program deals with training. It will show how to organize a continuing effort that will quickly make productive salesmen of the new men; help the steady performers improve their record; and teach all salesmen about new products, new selling methods, and new policies. Even if a company's sales program were completely static, it would still need a training system to improve the skills of those joining the team and to maintain the sales momentum of the present force. Rather than having a static condition, however, most sales managers find that change is the only constant, and that a broad and continuous training effort is essential if sales goals are to be met. The logical development of such a program follows a familiar pattern. The first step is to define the needs, the second is to appraise the team's present performance and qualifications, and the final action is to establish the type of mutual contribution by trainer and salesman that builds skills. A wide assortment of methods is available for both individual and group training, as shown in Exhibit 17. Proper construction of a unified program may call for all of these to be used, but that decision can be made only after the objectives are established.

Which Skills Are Needed?

In the preceding chapter, an ideal salesman was defined as one who understands his customer's business, has a good technical background in his customer's skill areas, and has complete knowledge of his own company's selling points and capabilities. If to that list can be added a talent for two-way communication, the result is a salesman who can and will succeed. The individual company must translate these broad requirements into an even more precise definition of the skills that are needed, and the training program should be based on the position guide that has already controlled the recruiting program. Exhibit 18 illustrates how the

Exhibit 17. Training methods and training needs.

| Training Methods | Training Needs | | | | |
| | Individual | | | Group | |
	Initial Uniform Training	Initial Special Training	Continuing Training Based on Performance	New Products, Sales Methods, Policies	Review and Stimulation
Standard package, including written and personal instruction					
Customized package to fit needs, including written and personal instruction					
Skilled individuals within company who can be used for training assignments					
Full-time trainer within the company					
Use of outside training and educational written programs					
Use of outside facilities, such as schools, professional and technical institutes					
Organized periodic local meetings					
Organized periodic major or national meetings					

Exhibit 18. The skills required to be a successful salesman of lawn and garden fertilizers and chemicals.

Product and Technical

Knowledge of company and competitive product formulations, including agronomic effect, amounts recommended, application techniques, and comparative costs and benefits of leading products of the three major producers.

Knowledge of local grasses, flowers, and vegetables (but not knowledge of market gardening or commercial farming). Knowledge of proper care and feeding, and some ability to diagnose common diseases and nutrient and climatic deficiencies.

Customer's Business

Knowledge of all lawn and garden wholesalers in the territory, their key personnel, lines carried, service and credit capability, major retail accounts sold by each one, and price and discount policy.

Knowledge of key retailers, decision makers, lines carried.

Understanding of and, ideally, practical experience in the operation of a lawn and garden center, a nursery, a hardware store, or a lawn care service.

Knowledge of golf course maintenance, equipment, and budget procedures.

Experience in inventory control, product display, and retail sales techniques.

Experience in developing continuing retail merchandising campaigns for lawn and garden products. Ability to make maximum use of advertising materials and assistance supplied by manufacturers.

Company Business

Ability to enter orders correctly, secure shipping dates, check on deliveries, and remedy customer complaints about shipping and service.

Ability to explain credit and billing procedure and insure prompt payment, to analyze customer problems, and to work with correct company department for quick solution.

Ability to handle product complaints quickly, settling minor ones on the spot according to policy, and submitting all needed facts on major ones.

Personal Traits

Ability to address groups of retailers, explaining company program and securing orders for products and commitments for merchandising support.

Experience in addressing user groups, such as garden clubs, golf course superintendents, and nurserymen.

---

position guide that appeared in Chapter 7 can be converted into an inventory of the talents needed for effective territory management.

Appraising Performance and Qualifications

Training programs start with a balance sheet, showing the assets the field salesmen already possess, the liabilities that must be converted into assets, and the talents that must be built or improved. Taking the example shown in Exhibit 18 as an illustration, the logical step after developing the list of skills required is for the salesman and his boss to agree on the level of ability that now exists and on the priorities for change. Perhaps the new salesman has been promoted from a sales administrative function; he knows company procedures thoroughly, but has no understanding of what it takes to operate a retail business profitably. Or he may already have been trained in agronomy, but in the laboratory, where he never addressed a group of people. The correct launching of a training program for each individual, and for the sales team by major units and as a whole, must include the appraisal of several factors.

Measuring the ability to handle the present job. One method of assessing present ability is to prepare a checklist, similar to those at the end of each chapter in this book, but listing the skills and talents needed for the present job. If each man is then asked to rate himself by such standards as "OK," "Needs some work," and "Key area for attention," he is giving a valuable insight into his own feeling of self-confidence. Whether the boss can make the same judgments depends on how well he knows the individual, but he can certainly agree or disagree with the rating the man has given himself. A mutually satisfactory balance sheet has then been developed that leads easily into a customized program to help one man do his job better.

Assessing the ability of a group to handle the present job is more difficult, but without such a judgment the sales manager cannot be sure that his training efforts are really correcting problems or improving performance. Veterans of any armed service can testify to the training programs that were repeated interminably, and to the education they received, whether they needed it or not. Sales training must be a reaction to a state of affairs, a filling of specific needs that have been determined by a current appraisal.

Perhaps the recent trend in orders has emphasized low-end, low-profit items, and the men's performance with premium products has declined. That's a specific training need. The list of new customers may be getting shorter each month, possibly an indication of stronger efforts by competitors to hold on to their accounts. Is the cause of the decline a pricing problem, a morale problem, or is the problem the fact that no one knows what the problem really is? A specific training program—perhaps a round table session, carefully moderated—may be the answer.

Measuring the ability to perform new tasks in existing markets. The market-oriented company is always making adjustments and improvements because its market segments are constantly changing. New or better products, revisions of sales and distribution channels, every move sets up a training requirement. Early identification of the need makes training simpler and more effective. The salesmen do not have the particular skill; they couldn't have, since the change had not taken place. Will they be trained before or after the fact? Fitting the training program to the field sales plan calls for the answer to the question, "What new duties must our sales force perform *in our present markets* during the coming year?" When the answer is clear, the correct method of imparting the new skill will be equally clear, and it will mean that the salesmen become confident and eager to take on the new task—rather than doubtful of their ability.

Measuring the ability to discharge entirely new, but planned, responsibilities. In addition to the periodic revision of present job duties, there are the moves into entirely new fields. The size of the "skill leap" must be measured and the necessary training system established. A single skill leap means keeping in touch with one market segment that is already being served. For example, if a manufacturer of kitchen and industrial cabinets enters the office furniture field, it is a single skill leap. He already knows how to make metal furniture; he has maintained his supply identity but is going after a new demand segment. The training problem is large, but not as great as if he were to take a double skill leap. Suppose he decided to begin the sale of office machines, initially made for him by another manufacturer. He has now jumped into both new supply and demand segments. His sales force doesn't know the product and doesn't know the market.

Sales forces are always being reorganized, sometimes for the better, and advance training improves the chance for success. At the same time, a careful analysis of the time and expense necessary to develop skilled field selling in a new business may make the company take another look at the project. Proper sales training is just as valid a startup expense as tooling and dies.

Assessing the willingness to work hard, efficiently, and in accordance with company objectives. A sales force is a team and, like any team, it responds to external pressures. After a busy season, there may be a general feeling that it's time to rest a while. When companies merge, there can often be confusion and even jealousy within the sales force that is unified only on paper and still hangs on to old loyalties. In all cases, progress toward the annual goals needs careful watching to determine if the sales force is turning in the performance expected of it. Naturally, the ability to judge working efficiency is tied closely to how well the tasks have been defined in terms of the concrete results to be achieved. "How's business?" must inevitably be answered with another question, "Compared to what?"

Preventing complacency at the managerial level. The well-established company must be on guard against poor performance by its executives, as well as by its salesmen and laborers. A full order book can tempt marketing management into believing that it needs only a restricted and unimaginative training program. A few manuals (frequently out of date), some unstructured visits at headquarters with whoever is available, and the new man can be sent to the field. There, a few days riding around with an experienced salesman and a brief introduction to his major customers make him a territory manager.

Group training can be just as glaring an example of management failure. The traditional Friday afternoon branch sales meeting grinds on week after week, so boring that even the local sales manager dreads attending his own creation. The annual sales meeting becomes a festive reunion, and the principal question is choosing the resort where it will be held, rather than what the objectives of the conference are. How wrong, and yet how common such an attitude is. What a waste of precious assets to come this far in the development of a complete field sales program, and not conceive and implement the best training program possible.

Establishing the Training Program

Individual Training

The opening inventory. As each new man is employed, he and his boss make an inventory of skills needed and skills present, and their action begins to pay handsome dividends immediately. The salesman has opened his mind by acknowledging that he will be more competent when he has acquired additional knowledge. The company has contributed to this positive attitude because it is demonstrating that he will not get a rigid, canned training course, but a personal one, carefully tailored to make the best use of his time. He will not waste days and hours on material he already knows, but neither will he get a quick once-over in those areas where he needs lots of help from experts.

The standard package. A uniform indoctrination package should be designed and given to each new sales employee. Properly done, it can increase his self-confidence and make him glad he joined the team. He needs to know about his company, his benefits, and his responsibilities. Standard reporting procedures must be learned, and he should meet those associates with whom he will be dealing. Will his initial training make him feel like an intruder, sitting in the conference room and reading a jumble of papers? Will his get-acquainted tour be a haphazard juggling of hasty visits, or will it be a planned sequence of information and demonstration that helps him understand how the company functions? Even so simple a device as a loose-leaf notebook, with an individually typed schedule and space for his notes, will make the new man feel that he is a welcome and important contributor to future profits.

The customized package. Equipping a salesman for his assignment now moves into the third and final step. His training needs have been established, and some of them have then been supplied by the standard package. Those that remain will be filled by a customized package, individually prepared and discussed with the man in advance. His concurrence means that he has agreed that when the proposed training is completed, he is equipped to handle his job and ready to go into the field.

Customized training often involves putting the salesman in the hands of those expert in specific work—the credit manager, an assembly foreman, or an experienced territory manager. The sales supervisor may delegate the specific teaching assignment, but he cannot delegate his larger responsibility for translating that knowledge into sales and profits. The teacher can be held accountable only for one thing—teaching what he knows. He has special knowledge, but he usually does not know how that knowledge is applied in the territory. All customized training must include frequent reviews by the new salesman and his boss, where the skill that has been learned is restated in terms of the field sales job.

The continuing individual training program. Personal direction, plus periodic reports, indicate to the supervisor how each of his salesmen is doing compared with his standard of performance. Continuing training should be designed to overcome problems when they are still small, to raise the salesman's overall performance level, and to prepare a man for new assignments. It ties directly to career development, a motivating force to be discussed in the next chapter. Whether the individual wants to remain a territory manager or become vice-president, he wants to be the best of his group. Poorly designed training can be a burden and can make the man feel that his performance must be substandard. Results-oriented training, on the other hand, convinces the man that the company wants him to succeed as much as he does.

Outside sources can often be used to help increase an individual's ability. The wide assortment of correspondence courses and the special short courses at schools and universities represent an efficient way to add to the territory manager's skills without taking him away from his customers for long periods. More and more industry, trade, and marketing groups have developed specific instruction programs, often with a certified graduate designation that enables the salesman to be more helpful to his accounts and to be recognized by them as having professional status.

Group Training

An organized training session for a group of salesmen usually has one of two purposes: to teach something new or to improve present performance by review and stimulation. Motivation plays so important a part in securing cooperation that it is often hard to tell whether the meeting is for education or for inspiration, and that's a good thing. Education should be stimulating, and a rousing pep talk carries little weight unless it also provides some new answers to old questions.

Teaching something new. The most common objectives of bringing a group together to learn a new skill include:

- Introducing a new product or the annual product line.
- Explaining the sales force's duties in a major new merchandising program.
- Capitalizing on competition's problems or blunting the other company's success.
- Developing new sales techniques for product customers or prospects.

Review and stimulation. The sales force also needs periodic revitalization through a combination of training and motivation. The training portion of the meeting can include:

- Refurbishing proven sales techniques or using new materials to make them even more effective.
- Improving operating practices, through discussion of current problems and agreement on improved methods of solving them.
- Increasing selling time and selling efficiency, through careful planning and better support for the territory manager.

Motivation convinces the salesman that he is capable of superior performance, that he has the tools he needs, and makes him want to hurry back to his assignment. Both aspects, review and stimulation, are critical. Too many sales forces have sat through dull technical meetings that left them confused and depressed. About as many other sales forces have left the hall to the sound of music and the exhortation of the sales manager, only to wonder at the airport what was really said and done to help them do their job.

Developing Effective Group Training

The cost of group training is staggering. As much as 10 percent of a salesman's annual working hours can be spent traveling to and attending meetings. Production costs, hotel and meal expense, and executive time run the bill still higher. Faced with the need to get his money's worth, the sales manager must scrutinize his training programs as carefully as his customers study their purchases from him. He is spending a lot of company money, much of it an invisible cost, and he requires full value. One training area that can cause a lot of trouble is the hazy definition of the results expected.

The "attentive man" approach. If a training program is less than a complete success, look first at the definition of objectives. Chances are that the purpose of the exercise was not really clear, or that too many goals had been established—a common failing when salesmen come from long distances and every department wants a crack at them. Since the broadcast was muddled, the reception was equally poor. Sometimes the objective can be clear, but badly off course. Many an annual sales meeting has been conceived to "put on a bigger and better show than last year"—hardly a training objective and a very doubtful motivational goal except for the headquarters types producing the meeting.

The attentive man approach shifts the spotlight away from those responsible for organizing the meeting and focuses it on those who attend. It moves the time frame forward, from the present planning session to the moment when the future meeting is ending. It visualizes an attentive man who has just walked out of the last or only session and asks him, "What are you going to do as a result of what you heard and saw?" The answer that he should give becomes the training objective. The meeting will now be based on the results it is designed to produce, rather than on what the company's managers want to get off their chest.

For example, a frequent reason for a group meeting is to introduce new or improved models that strengthen the existing product lines. The conventional approach would set as the objective: to instruct the sales force about the new models and their sales features. The meeting schedule would probably include engineering data, critical analysis of competitive products, discussion of warranty claims, and an inspirational "go get 'em." It would not be a bad meeting at all. Several salesmen would assure management that it was "the finest sales meeting I ever attended," and there would be an encouraging flow of new orders.

The attentive man approach takes the same training assignment and handles it differently. The company wants its man to say at the end of the meeting, "I know exactly where I can get new customers with these new models and where I can increase sales to present accounts; and I know how to get the order." Now the results desired are stated in human terms. No longer is the aim solely to educate; it is to help each man create a selling campaign. This meeting will concentrate on customer needs, will show how to make progress through the steps of a sale, and how to get that first order from new accounts. Both meetings have many common features, but the angle of development is different. So is the success that follows.

The attentive man approach is especially necessary for the annual sales meeting or other major periodic get-togethers. Without realizing it, those who control the session can stray far from the true sales training course. How many meetings have been held to impress the president, or to prove how well the marketing group can use new visual aids techniques? Other large meetings will emphasize negatives — cost cutting, halts in expansion until profits improve, demands to improve sales performance. The sales manager may think the effect is salutary, but he is not listening to the attentive man. The good salesman may say, when asked what action he will take as a result of the get-together, "I'm going to look for another job, because I just wasted my time at a sales meeting that had no application to me. I'm afraid it's symptomatic of the advancement opportunities in this company."

Other Training Techniques

Periodic local meetings. Planning, organizing, and leading are three basic management functions, but all too often they are glaringly absent in periodic local sales meetings. The regular assembly of the sales force has degenerated into a session at which individuals are publicly raked over the coals, or it has become an absolute bore. Starting with such basic questions as "Why hold them?," the manager needs to make sure that each local sales meeting is results oriented and worth the several hundred dollars of lost selling time. The same attentive man approach will work for small groups, and the objective of the meeting can be spelled out with great clarity.

Outside services and agencies. Experts from outside the company can be hard to control and often say things that make management cringe. This independence, however, increases their credibility and usually more than offsets any shock waves created. In addition to sending a sales group to a school or to a trade association conference, the manager can bring one or more speakers to the company's central meeting or schedule them into a series of local training sessions. Usually the outside expert will have more than enough knowledge, except about the company and its problems and challenges. By using the attentive man approach it becomes easy to direct the activities of the visitor into helpful channels. He should not be told what to say. He should be told what action the group ought to take as a result of hearing him. The objective is not to get the expert to do something, but to get him to make others do something.

Group self-training. A teacher isn't essential to the learning process, and a sales trainer isn't essential to sales training. A group can educate itself if it has a clear goal and sufficient knowledge of the subject. The exchange of ideas on how to solve common problems is a tested technique to improve the performance of a sales team. The moderator must keep the group on course, or else the storytelling starts, the sales successes are dramatized, and the meeting falls apart.

Self-training goes hand in hand with self-examination. One very effective technique is to periodically review the sales job, bringing the men together to discuss such topics as: How has your job changed in the last few years? What results are you trying to produce, and how can you be supported more effectively? What have you found to be the most effective way to develop your skill in . . . ?

Training the Supervisors

In the preceding chapter the dilemma that faces the sales supervisor was pointed out. Newly appointed to the managerial level, he may have doubts about his ability and a clear need for specialized training. Yet he may be unable to admit his problem to others. If the same method of identifying skills and taking inventory is used for supervisors as for salesmen, a good beginning has been made in organizing an effective training process. The response to the inventory must be completely individualized, and it must be of the highest quality. What does it matter if a few thousand dollars are spent to develop the talents of a man who is now a major factor in attaining the company's profit goals?

Much has been written about the failure to expand training to include supervisors and managers, and much has been done to correct the problem. One of the best techniques is to set an example. If the field sales manager takes the lead in self-improvement, his supervisors will lose their inhibitions and freely agree that they too can improve themselves. On the other hand, the sales manager who is too busy to learn the intricacies of a new product, or to attend a well-organized industry workshop, is signaling clearly that he considers training a waste of time for himself and those others who, having risen above the rank of salesman, now very obviously have all the answers to all the problems.

Administrative Training

The training of clerical, warehouse, and service employees began when brief position guides were developed with their help. Even at that early stage, the attention of each person was focused on the skills he or she needed. Thus the process of self-training, of watching others work, and of asking for help became results oriented rather than aimless. To this should be added a formal program to develop latent talents or to build new ones. The field sales manager will often find that he can call on other departments for assistance; after all, the controller wants the invoices typed correctly just as much as the sales department does. The theme that should run through the administrative training program is "sales support." Employees should be skilled in their work, but they have their jobs solely to strengthen the sales effort. Technical competence is fine, but not if it is wrapped in a personality or attitude that antagonizes customers or fails to build a selling atmosphere.

Summary

A field sales manager who fails to organize a complete sales training program has hurt himself, his men, and his company. If he does not develop his sales force's skills, he will find himself resorting to bullying, harsh criticism, and dictatorial discipline in an attempt to gain performance through fear. If he abdicates his responsibility and lets the sales training group or the product managers take charge, he will find that his men no longer think of him as their personal leader. On the other hand, if he enlists the help of others but retains the control and the accountability for success, he is performing his job just the way he should. No one expects him to be an expert in all matters — technical, administrative, or production — but everyone expects him to be an expert in building a skilled sales force. The following checklist will help to determine what training needs must be filled, what actions can be delegated, and what management control is needed to make the sales force better and better and better.

Checklist No. 8
Developing Skills

TOPIC	OK	NEEDS SOME WORK	KEY AREA FOR ATTEN- TION	DOES NOT APPLY

Defining the Need

1. The need for continuous sales training is recognized, and we have a systematic and effective program under the direction of the field sales manager.

——— ——— ——— ———

2. The skills required for each type of sales position have been described (as illustrated in Exhibit 18), including product and technical, those involving the customer's business and the company's business, and desirable personal traits.

——— ——— ——— ———

Each salesman, and the major sales force units, have been appraised in terms of

Checklist No. 8
(Continued)

TOPIC	OK	NEEDS SOME WORK	KEY AREA FOR ATTEN-TION	DOES NOT APPLY
3. Ability to handle the present (or proposed) job.	___	___	___	___
4. Ability to perform new tasks in existing markets.	___	___	___	___
5. Ability to discharge entirely new but planned responsibilities.	___	___	___	___
6. Willingness to work hard, efficiently, and in accordance with company objectives.	___	___	___	___

Individual Training

7. A comprehensive training program has been developed for new salesmen and is operating efficiently.	___	___	___	___
8. Each man has participated in the design of his individual training program and is convinced that he will benefit from it.	___	___	___	___
9. A standard package that tells about the company, the benefits, and the regular operating procedures has been designed and is enthusiastically communicated to each new employee.	___	___	___	___
10. A customized package is constructed for each new salesman. It gives him the skills he needs and does not waste time on those he already has.	___	___	___	___
11. Each salesman receives periodic counseling on his performance and is encouraged to develop his skills with company and outside programs.	___	___	___	___
12. Written records show the specific and continuing training that each man is				

Checklist No. 8
(Continued)

TOPIC	OK	NEEDS SOME WORK	KEY AREA FOR ATTEN- TION	DOES NOT APPLY
receiving (by whatever name given to *training*).	___	___	___	___

Group Training

	OK	NEEDS SOME WORK	KEY AREA FOR ATTEN- TION	DOES NOT APPLY
13. The need to learn a new skill or technique is identified in advance, and an organized program teaches men how to do a job before they are required to do it.	___	___	___	___
14. Periodic meetings are scheduled only when the benefit outweighs the cost. There are no "must" meetings.	___	___	___	___
15. The "attentive man" approach is used to make sure that each meeting has clear objectives and that it is results oriented.	___	___	___	___
16. Local group meetings are carefully organized. The central office supplies appropriate material. The salesmen think local meetings help them and are worth the time.	___	___	___	___
17. Opportunities to use outside services and agencies have been fully explored, and an effective program has been set up.	___	___	___	___
18. Self-training is widely used, and employees are able to formulate their own answers to problems and challenges.	___	___	___	___
19. In building an effective sales training program we have not neglected our supervisors, and a strong, complete program is operating effectively.	___	___	___	___

Checklist No. 8
(Continued)

TOPIC	OK	NEEDS SOME WORK	KEY AREA FOR ATTEN-TION	DOES NOT APPLY

Administrative Employees

20. Experts in and out of the company have been consulted on training for administrative employees, and a sound, comprehensive program appropriate to the need is operating effectively. ___ ___ ___ ___

Summary

21. In summary, we have a continuing training program that is based on customer needs. It brings new men to profitable levels quickly, helps steady performers improve their record, and teaches all salesmen about new products, new selling methods, and new policies. ___ ___ ___ ___

9 / Motivating Superior Performance

THE final step in Phase 3 is the development of a series of programs that will make each person on the sales team perform to the limit of his ability. Alone most of the time, accountable principally to his own conscience, a salesman needs reassurance and stimulation. To motivate means to incite to action, and the key components in motivating a sales force are compensation, incentives, and career development. The right kind of motivation encourages day-in, day-out field selling effort and higher levels of accomplishment. Failure to create proper motivation has penalized many companies heavily, including some giant ones. Annual turnover may be as high as 35 percent, and costs for finding and training men are excessive. Many of their best salesmen have left to become the supervisors and managers of other sales forces. Establishment of a sound reward and stimulation package is therefore not simply a goodwill gesture to the salesman. It is designed to hold the best men and to keep them active, for the benefit of the entire company.

Compensation

When the structure of the sales force was set, a lot of the compensation questions were settled. Company-controlled sales forces usually are paid salaries, plus incentives, and independent contractors earn commissions—with exceptions in both cases. The degree of experience and talent needed for the sales job dictates the level of compensation. In today's inflationary climate, the employee benefit program is assuming even more importance than ever; it can remove the fear of heavy current expenses or insure a rising value for whatever is put aside. Some form of added compensation, either as commission or bonus, should supplement a salesman's fixed salary. Finally, compensation includes those privileges that apply to a position or to an individual which are often a powerful motivating force.

Salary or Guaranteed Income

When a company agrees to pay a salary, it demonstrates that it is confident a salesman will succeed, and that it is not withholding payment of a reward until after a sale has been made. The company has decided that the key objective is to get the man working as hard as he can, with a minimum of distractions, and that a guaranteed income is one step toward reaching that objective. Certainly there can be drawbacks: men can coast along, performance can be slipshod. In some businesses a salary can be seen as a limitation on earnings, rather than as a guarantee, and straight commission is by far the best arrangement. For many companies, however, the foundation of the motivational package is the base salary, and its popularity is proof of its effectiveness.

The tests of whether or not a salary or guaranteed income is best for the man and the company include: Does he need a salary to cover living expenses and to eliminate the day-to-day financial worries that decrease his effectiveness? Is his success hard to measure in terms of actual sales? Is his work principally technical sales support, or does he work with headquarters personnel and not buyers? Is the company asking him to develop a new opportunity with little or no initial sales volume and uncertain growth?

If the answer is yes to any of these questions, the best motivation base is salary or guaranteed income. If at all possible, it should be supplemented by the opportunity to earn added rewards.

Contingent Compensation

When a salesman receives extra pay for specific accomplishments, the motivating force is immediate, direct, and strong. Because of this, any plan for contingent compensation must be carefully drawn. It will incite action, and only advance planning can make sure that the action is consistent with company objectives. Commissions, overrides, and performance bonuses are the most common vehicles, and should meet the following tests:

Make binding, measurable commitments. Unless the person who is supposed to act is absolutely clear on exactly what he must do, and exactly what extra income he will earn, the motivating force drops or disappears. Put the plan in writing and fulfill it completely, without change or subsequent "interpretation."

Avoid discretionary plans. A plan that bases the reward on a subjective rating, or on the attainment of some goal beyond the salesman's control, is a defective plan. The man wants to be rated on his performance as he sees it or, hopefully, as the facts prove. He does not want another person to control his reward. And he definitely does not want to be told that he will get a bonus if the company reaches a certain profit level. Profit sharing may be fine for other employees, but only because they need to work as a team, or because individual success cannot be measured. If the salesman has a set goal, reward him in relation to his personal achievement.

Make it easy to calculate. The best commission or bonus plan is one that can be translated into a specific amount of money by the salesman, in his head, just before the call. If he has to wait for the accounting report to see how much he made, the plan is too complicated. He should be able to say, "My sales objective on this call is an order for x, and when I get it I will earn y in commission."

Pay promptly. The position guide has spelled out the salesman's responsibilities; pay him when they are performed. If his job is to get orders, pay him on acceptance, not on shipment or on receipt of customer's check. The amount at risk is small, and the motivational gain is tremendous. Pick the earliest realistic occasion to reward the accomplishment.

Make any change a matter of mutual agreement. Salesmen are often suspicious of changes in compensation plans, and with good reason. A higher quota, a smaller territory, or a revision of commission rates all too frequently takes dollars out of the man's pocket. When it is necessary to make changes, he should be involved, not merely informed. If commissions are to be reduced, motivation can be maintained by increasing the salary. One good rule of thumb is to convert one-third of the difference to base salary. If a man earns $10,000 in commission he will not be happy to move to a tougher territory, at the company's request, where only $7,000 in commission is likely. Chances are a $1,000 salary increase will rekindle his ambition, since the added amount is permanent, increases the value of his benefit program, and raises him on the organization ladder.

Be sure the plan is consistent with company objectives. The classic case of an inconsistent compensation plan involves the company that paid its salesmen a straight commission, based on sales volume alone, even though its products had widely varying profit margins. Seasonal selling objectives can also produce inconsistencies. One company wanted orders for November and December, both of them slack production months. Commissions stopped, however, when a salesman hit 120 percent of annual quota. As a result, if a salesman sold a unit in the last weeks of the year, he might not earn any commission. In addition, it would be a sale borrowed from the following year (when he would be back on commission) and might also be used by the company to raise his annual quota. It was totally against the salesman's interest to do what the company wanted done. Any compensation plan needs to be tested against the question, "What will it make the salesman exert every effort to do, and is that action the best from the company's viewpoint?"

The Standard of Performance

Anyone who has been a field salesman knows the importance of individual standards of performance. Every territory manager or supervisor wants to feel that he is contributing his share to the success of his company. He wants to be rewarded on the basis of what he has accomplished in relation to the task that has been set. He needs to know, "What constitutes doing a good job?" The man on the production line can operate his machine to its capacity, the girl in the office can type invoices all day long, and each knows that a good job has been done.

In the territory, however, the salesman is confronted daily with the fact that he gets only a small share of the available business, and that the total sales volume of his competitors far exceeds his own. There are many fine accounts that he is unable to sell. Does this mean that he is a failure? Perhaps he can't get all the business, but how much should he get? Unless a standard of performance is set, these nagging questions can destroy his self-confidence, make him critical of company and product, and finally drive him away. With his task defined, he can measure his own success, and the company can reward him fairly for what he accomplishes.

Setting individual standards. The position guide has established the results expected from each and every salesman on the team. If, for example, there are 20 salesmen of builders' hardware, the work done in each territory will be similar, and the goals will be the same in principle, but not in quantity or priority. The standard of performance recognizes that each man and each territory are different, and sets individual levels of accomplishment that stretch the man's ability and yet are realistic. The competition, the number and value of the present accounts, and the selling ability of the salesman are measured against the total potential. With the participation of the territory manager, standards are established, defining a "good job" in terms of

- Annual sales volume, divided by major time periods or product groups
- Selling profit or target margin to be obtained (in some cases the salesman sells only at the published price)
- Territory expense and local funds for selling programs and customer support
- Other financial standards, such as average accounts receivable outstanding or value of inventory in territory warehouses
- Sales accomplishments, such as new customers to be gained, training programs to be conducted, or new products introduced

An individual standard of performance carries the concept of a field sales program down to the territorial level. It makes each salesman a manager, responsible for organizing the same type of plan for his area as the sales manager develops for the whole company. It is an essential component of the motivational program. When fair standards of performance are set, men work more effectively and are rewarded commensurately with their success. Without his own individual standard, the man in the field is a worker instead of a manager, and the compensation plan degenerates into a discretionary nightmare of unequal rewards, unhappy salesmen, and unattained sales goals.

Company Benefit Programs

What were at one time called fringe benefits have now become such a major part of the compensation package that their cost to the company often exceeds 25 percent of an employee's salary. And yet, many companies are almost apologetic for the generous programs they offer. Advertisements of vacant positions will refer to competitive benefits, or interviewers will say that their program is as good as other good companies'. A far more positive approach is needed when talking to salesmen.

The first step is to reduce the many company booklets and tables into an easy-to-read guide for prospective salesmen. They want to know about pensions, insurance, and the basic advantages the company offers, but in clear, short sentences; the details can come later. In addition, they need to get answers to some special questions. What insurance protection does the man's family have when he travels on company business, and does day-to-day territory work constitute travel? Is he protected if his wife has an accident while driving the company car? Will the company's contribution to his retirement fund be based on salary alone, or do commissions and bonuses also count? Proper presentation of the company's benefit programs increases the pulling power of the compensation plan, and helps to attract the stable, family type of man who is often the backbone of the field force.

One company went a step further and recognized the fact that most salesmen occasionally think of being in business for themselves, either alone or with a few associates. Taking a few examples of annual earnings by its salesmen, it calculated the dollar value of the company's contribution to the many benefit plans.

It then pointed out that an individual might have to pay much more for the same protection and might even have some income tax liability. The resulting analysis clearly demonstrated that there was far more to the compensation package than salary and commission, and that a man would have to do very well indeed in his own business to have the effective income that he could enjoy as a territory manager.

Privileges and Perquisites

A perquisite is defined as something in addition to wages and salary; it is also the foundation of much business humor. Jokes about the carpeted versus the uncarpeted office or the key to the executive washroom have obscured a basic and very true behavioral concept. Rank does have privileges, and those who hold rank want to exercise their privileges. The clear definition of privileges and perquisites is especially important for the sales force; most employees do not spend company money, drive company cars, or have direct contact with customers, but salesmen do. The wise employer spells out its policies, putting them in writing whenever possible. Some of the areas that often cause conflict and unhappiness unless clarified are:

- Operation of the company car by members of the salesman's family. Use of the car for vacations. Amount to be paid the company for personal use.
- Expense account guidelines, especially regarding meals and tips. What expenses can be charged if the salesman takes his wife with him on a trip.
- Business entertainment expenses, particularly club memberships.
- Business expenses, such as subscriptions to technical journals, attendance at industry meetings, and the hiring of stenographic services.

Not all privileges must be given to all salesmen. Some companies furnish more expensive cars to their senior territory managers. Others restrict club memberships to supervisors or to those men who deal with the central offices of large customers. Attendance at a convention can be a reward for those who have attained their sales goals. In a sense, privileges can also be considered as part of the incentives portion of the motivation package, in addition to the role they play in compensation. The important point is that the company must consciously use the extension of privileges as a spur to increased selling effort. If the policy is not clear, or if the extra benefits are dispensed begrudgingly, a valuable motivating factor has been thrown away.

Designing the Total Compensation Package

When a complete field sales program is built step by step, it becomes much easier to develop an effective and stimulating compensation package. As the field sales needs are defined, the type of man who must be attracted becomes clear, and so does the basic payment plan. New men in their first selling job rarely want to work for straight commission. Experienced, successful territory managers want to be paid more than a salary. When it is time to define the contingent compensation, the clear statement of company objectives makes it possible to design a commission or bonus plan that meets all the tests already listed. In the best sales compensation packages, individuals earn individual rewards; the team concept all too often means that the company cannot measure each man's performance, a sad commentary on the sales program. Finally, the many benefit programs and privileges can be presented in a way that will attract the type of man the company must have in the field. A total package has been developed systematically, by defining the needs and the buying motives of the salesman, and then filling those needs in a way that supports the basic company objectives.

A Few Thoughts on Compensation

Avoid group or anniversary raises. An increase in compensation should be a reward for outstanding performance or a stimulus to increased effort. It is often best given immediately after a big sale or when sales are very low and selling problems unusually tough. A raise is a direct communication of confidence from boss to subordinate — or it should be.

If the increase is tied to a recurring date (fiscal year, end of season), or if a large group receives increases at the same time, the individual motivation is lost. The higher pay may appear to be the company's grudging acknowledgment that the help must be paid more or they will desert. The sales manager's goal is to convince his men that each salesman is rewarded as a result of an individual appraisal of his performance. Group increases promote the idea that everybody who can hold his job will get some of the "kitty," and that there is little point in striving for superior sales results.

The ideal arrangement is to incorporate all the proposed raises in the annual field sales program and to secure advance approval. The actual awarding of the increase is then timed to have the maximum motivational effect. Giving a man a raise just before he leaves on vacation brings smiles to the whole family. The salesman who has tried hard but lost a big order can be recharged when he gets an increase instead of a reprimand. In all cases, each man feels that he has been treated as an individual, not just another member of the group.

Consider a raise on starting day. One very successful sales manager, and a great builder of human relations, used a special technique when he hired a potentially outstanding salesman. He knew that a good man would soon wonder about an increase, but that it was hard to secure company approval until a year or so had elapsed. He prepared the employment papers with the next higher (but still authorized) salary level listed for the company records. On the day the new salesman reported for work, he would be told that the sales manager was so confident of his ability that he was giving him his first raise now. It's easy to picture the enthusiasm with which the new territory manager tackled his assignment, then rushed home to tell his family what his new employer thought of him.

Monitor the first paycheck. Few things will upset a new man more than a delay in receiving his first paycheck. He shouldn't worry, but he does. It doesn't help to tell him after the fact that the personnel department was slow in processing his papers or that there was a question about deductions. Many wise sales managers arrange to have the first check delivered to them in advance of the regular payday, then send it to the salesman with a brief, hand-written note expressing realistic but upbeat appraisal of sales results to date. A potential negative situation has been converted into a motivational plus.

Incentives and Contests

The competitive value of incentive programs has been amply demonstrated, and almost every sales program contains some special features designed to stimulate extra effort. Along with the positive value of contests go problems, particularly if time-tested rules are violated. The sales manager must develop company-wide programs, and also institute or encourage the simple local ones that weld a small team more closely together. He should be guided by several principles.

Be brief. Rarely can a contest hold attention for more than 90 days; a 30-day period is ideal. If the contest is a lengthy one, attention flags, or the winners become evident too early, or the stigma of being a nonwinner festers too long. It would have been better had the contest never been held.

Be fair. No two territories, branches, or regions are alike. The home office may feel that in its wisdom it has allowed for these differences by adjusting quotas or tasks, but the field force seldom agrees. Competition between individuals or units is about as dangerous as advertisements that use humor, sex, or politics — many people can be angered and react negatively. "Every man a winner" should be the goal.

Money talks. Merchandise and travel incentives have their place, but nothing has the universal appeal of money, especially if the company agrees to make the prize a "net" award, by taking care of the added tax burden. Travel awards appeal to the man on top who has a high income, married children, and a full wardrobe for himself and his wife. For the rising salesman the same award can be a deterrent as he thinks of baby-sitters, school schedules, and new clothes. When in doubt, give money.

Don't substitute a temporary incentive for a sound compensation plan. One of the benefits of systematically developing a complete field sales program is the accurate definition of the type of man needed and the income that must be offered to attract him. The salesman is worthy of his hire for attaining his standard of performance, and the salary and commission plan must be complete and amply rewarding. Opportunities to win extra cash, merchandise, or special recognition should supplement and not replace the basic compensation package. A contest award should be a *plus*, not an "in lieu of."

Don't substitute an incentive or contest for a sound selling program. "Why do we need it?" should be asked whenever a contest is proposed. If the reason lies in product shortcomings, inadequate selling tools, or noncompetitive pricing, a special incentive is not the solution. The best plan for both the salesman and the company is to solve the basic problems and thereby make the sales task attainable. After that is done, a well-timed contest can spur the men on and make the changes even more effective.

Don't use a standard incentive package; customize it. Many effective contest formats have been organized by companies specializing in salesmen's incentive programs. They are easy to use; almost too easy. If a contest is worth its cost, it is also worth the effort needed to personalize the basic package. A "Sales Safari" or "Sales Round-Up" theme can be a good foundation, but the man in the territory wants to feel that the contest is related to *his individual selling situation*, and that the rewards have been scaled correctly. Incentive companies can do a lot of the work, but the sales manager must do his share to make it his contest.

Recognizing Individual Accomplishment

We all want recognition, and salesmen thrive on it. It is not enough to be able to tell himself that he is meeting his standard of performance, or even to have the boss tell him so. He wants others — especially his customers, prospects, and fellow salesmen — to know it. Many companies have established programs to recognize individual accomplishment. If carefully organized, these programs can increase sales and have a positive effect on the whole field force. Improperly handled, a recognition program will embarrass the recipient and turn the rest of the sales force off.

The "Man of the Year" award. An all too common way to recognize sales achievement is the designation of an individual or a unit as the best in its group. Branch X may win the president's cup for May or Salesman Y will be acclaimed the Salesman of the Year.

Chances are that the program is a net loss. True, there is a winner, but the award only emphasizes that every other person or group is a loser and publicly labels them as having done a less effective job than the victor (in the company's view).

What does a periodic winner program really accomplish? Will the victor work smarter or harder? He is probably close to the limit already. Will the rest of the team work smarter or harder? Possibly, but there's more chance of resentment and frustration and a drop in effort. Convinced that the rules are unfair and that their efforts are not given proper credit, the rest of the sales force resorts to criticizing the winner and the company that chose him.

An even more disastrous version of the periodic contest is the negative award. The "Lemon of the Month," passed from branch to branch, is really only a crude symbol of management failure at the home office, and not a proof of deficiency at the local level. Sales managers who are trying to make their men feel like responsible territory managers cringe at such farces as having sales team A (the winners) eat steak at the annual sales meeting, while sales team B (the losers, and a thoroughly frustrated group) eat hamburger.

The correct solution of course is a program that recognizes individual accomplishment and permits every man or unit to win, if the job is done. The President's Club, the 100 Percenters, or the Outstanding Branch Award gives everyone an opportunity for recognition, and avoids the tensions that arise when victory for one must be interpreted as defeat for all others. Better performance on the job cannot be attributed to the award alone. Clear definition of objectives, sympathetic counseling, and dynamic leadership mean far more than the plaque on the wall. If, however, the award program will be more than a two-month brainstorm (to be replaced by some other hot idea), if the basis for winning is seen by all as fair and attainable, and if the rest of the team will not react negatively, then an award program perhaps may have merit. If there is any doubt, drop the idea.

Career Development

The final step in the motivation process is to make sure that the company keeps its best men and that they become the foundation on which expansion is built. Turnover is the bane of field selling. Hiring, training, and supervising a new man for six months must cost a minimum of $10,000; if he leaves, it has all been wasted. The out-of-pocket loss is only one aspect, and often a small one. Had the territory been well manned, and had the sales supervisor been able to spend more time with his experienced producers, the company's sales and earning would have been far higher than the dismal results that caused the relatively new man to leave or to be fired.

And what about the unrealized profits from those territories where the fire has gone out of the local salesman and performance is far below standard? What is to be done about the man who is at a dead end? He knows that after several years' service, his earnings are about as high as they will go; he has been passed over for promotion or has turned down the relocation it would involve. Where is his incentive to strive for higher and higher levels of performance?

Career Development for All

Turnover cannot be eliminated by a program of career development for all salesmen, but it can be reduced. Career development alone will not make every senior salesman jump in the car bright and early every morning, but it is a positive stimulant. All that is meant by career development is to help the salesman decide what he wants to be, and then help him get there. Some men seek advancement, and the company has the choice of aiding them in achieving their goal or of seeing them leave. Other men want the satisfaction that comes from building their own territory and managing it year in and year out; but they need rewards and recognition if they are to keep the spark of competitive selling alive.

Career development and promotions. Building a reserve of promotable men involves measuring the demand and supply, developing special skills, and creating individualized compensation plans. Analysis of the demand comes first, for only through a balance between candidates and openings can there be an orderly progression in each man's career development. Underestimating the demand forces the company to go outside for managers and disillusions those who hope for advancement in the future. Overestimating the demand and hiring too many outstanding candidates is a familiar problem. Business is full of top-flight managers who got tired of waiting for one man's retirement to start the game of musical chairs through the organization; they left and won promotion elsewhere.

The supply of promotable salesmen can often be controlled by realistically maintaining a "development list" of potential managers already on the team. If the company is in the fortunate position of being two-deep in backup men for each major sales job, it needs to switch its recruiting efforts to attract the strong sales types who want to remain in territory work. A development list, even if only in the sales manager's head, also helps him to test his promotable men by special assignment and to improve their skills by special training.

Successful career development requires candid, personal communication. Some managers believe that telling a man he is scheduled for promotion breeds complacency and weakens control over his activity; frequently the real problem is insecurity on the manager's part. The promotable man knows that he is good at his work, and he wants to know what to expect in the future, and when. He will extend himself gladly, handling extra duties or studying nights and weekends, if he sees clearly how it will benefit him. The company should be equally interested in getting a commitment from him. It does not want to train him for a position only to find that his plan all along has been to move to another company or industry.

The third aspect of developing promotable men is compensation, and the message is don't be penny-wise and pound-foolish. Standard compensation packages may not fit the best candidates for promotion, and the central payment objective is to make sure that the man stays with the company until the opportunity matures. When this means a departure from established plans, so be it. If the man is worth keeping he is also worth special treatment. The extra cost, viewed against the potential of years of superior sales management, is next to nothing.

Parallel development for experienced salesmen. "Why do I have to take a promotion and a transfer to increase my earnings? Why can't you pay me more to manage this territory; you say I'm one of the best men on the team." It's not easy to give a good answer that makes sense for the man and the company. Traditionally, business operates on the concept that each job has an earnings range, and that the way to make more money is to get promoted. At the same time, market-oriented companies recognize that the strongest or weakest link in the whole marketing chain can be the man in the territory. It needs to keep its good men working where they are already effective; it cannot lose the best salesmen through unrealistic policies. Parallel development attempts to solve this very common problem by giving the territory salesman an opportunity to grow as much in his present job as if he moved into the supervisory ranks.

The three ingredients of a program of parallel development are compensation, recognition, and security. The man who wants to stay in the territory does not expect to earn a vice-president's income, but he knows that he is as valuable as a supervisor, or even a branch manager, and he expects to be in the same earnings bracket. If, for example, a district manager can earn $18,000 to $25,000, the company will not get the best out of its senior salesmen if their ceiling is $12,000. In addition to compensation, parallel development stresses recognition. The company invites its best men to its planning sessions, seeks their counsel, and debates alternatives with them. Visible differences separate the senior territory manager from the rest of the team; he has a different title, perhaps a more expensive automobile, he attends meetings of company officials and customers as a respected participant.

Even though he is making the money he thinks he should earn, and knows that he is recognized for his contributions, the program can founder on a problem that grows with the man's years of service — insecurity. What will happen if some "new broom" comes in at the top? Will his high income make him a prime candidate for separation in an economy drive? Will the managers of tomorrow recognize his value, or think he is coasting along? Parallel development sets up safeguards, ranging from employment contracts to informal commitments, to insure that the senior salesman can have the job, right where he wants it, and as long as he wants it. The only provision is that the mutually agreed-to standard of performance be met.

Contrast this happy situation with what goes on in many sales forces. Look through 20 letters received in response to an advertisement for a salesman, and pick out the ones from experienced men. The recurring theme will be the search for a change "for more income," "because I have reached the top salary for my present

Exhibit 19. Motivating superior performance with a complete compensation and career development program.

December 12

Mr. James Richards
Territory Manager
Albuquerque

Dear Jim:

You and I have had another excellent review of your accomplishments and the company's plans, and I'm glad we agree on what can be expected next year from the Albuquerque territory.

The standard of performance that we arrived at together includes the following objectives:

a. Total Sales Volume

1st six months	$240,000
2nd six months	290,000
Yearly total	$530,000

b. Product Sales

Tractors--Models YA and 2H	50
Tractors--Model YB	15

c. Prices
You will sell at published distributor prices, except where you have advance approval from me to quote a lower price.

d. Territory Operating Expense
Your total expenses, not including your compensation, but including travel, office, and warehouse costs, should not exceed $14,000, a 6% increase over this year's total.

e. Your average month-end warehouse stock of tractors, accessories and parts should not exceed $90,000.

f. Six new dealers are to be established, four of them in the southern half of your territory.

g. Our new series of technical training films will be ready by March 1, and you will hold a minimum of three meetings per month with dealers and users, aiming for at least 25 participants at each meeting. The company will pay for lunch, cocktails, and dinner at each meeting.

When you attain these objectives, you will be contributing your share to the attainment of the company's goals.

In addition to the new base salary which I was happy to tell you about when we met, you can earn additional compensation as follows:

2% on all shipments over 80% of the amount shown in (a) above ($530,000).

An additional 1% of the invoice value of all sales of the Model YB tractor.

The company has improved its benefit program again, and its value to you is increasing steadily. Your participation in the retirement plan will now be based on your total salary and commission earnings, rather than on salary alone. The company's contribution will be approximately $750 during the coming year. You have said you wish to continue to participate in the stock ownership plan. You may set aside 5% of your total salary and commission earnings, and the company will contribute one-half that sum to purchase stock.

You and your family will continue to have the protection of our medical plan and the new higher benefits. You will contribute $180 and the company will contribute $270. You may use your company automobile for recreational and shopping activities and for your vacation. Your wife is authorized to drive the car, but no other person is. The company expects that you will replace the gasoline used for personal driving.

We discussed your career with our company, and you continue to be one of those who we believe can assume greater responsibility. It seems now that we will be able to offer you a supervisory position in three years' time, and you have said that this fits in well with your personal plans and with the schooling of your children. We also reviewed the new or increased skills needed for the company's expansion and for your continued growth. You are going to take the University's special accounting course for business managers, and next summer you will attend the annual profit planning workshop at company headquarters. In addition, we will try to enroll you in the Sales Supervisor's Course given once a year. Jim Blake will send you a number of books to study in the coming months in preparation for the course.

Jim, I'm glad you're on my team, and I know I can count on you for the same consistent sales effort you have put forth in the last four years. I will be seeing you in late January, and hope that by then you will have some dealer prospects qualified to the point that we can have definitive talks with them and sign franchise agreements.

Sincerely,

Bill

William Hopkins

position," or, worst of all, "because the company is paying new men almost as much as they pay me." Surely within that group are skilled men who want to continue in their present work and who are profit producers; the system, however, is against them, and so the company will lose a valuable asset.

Motivating Superior Performance

Exhibit 19 illustrates how the three factors of compensation, incentives and contests, and parallel development can be combined to motivate a salesman to outstanding performance. The letter that is used as an example confirms all the major aspects of the relationship between the man and his boss and, through the boss, his company. The salesman has already discussed this year's accomplishments and next year's challenges; the agreed standard of performance is spelled out clearly. He knows what his salary is and when he will earn commissions, the amount of which he can calculate exactly. He is fully informed about the benefit programs the company has established and how much the company contribution increases his effective income.

The sales manager's happy position. The market-oriented company now has the sales force it deserves. The best type of salesmen have been chosen, given well-defined assignments, and trained to handle their duties efficiently. They are stimulated by a sound combination of financial and personal motivations, and they know what is expected of them and what their reward will be. It is a field force to be proud of, and already is stronger and more dynamic than most of its competition. But the program is not yet complete. The next key question is, "What will the salesman do when he meets the buyer face-to-face?" Before turning to that subject, the sales manager may want to check the effectiveness of his motivation program by completing the following checklist. He is then ready for Phase 4—providing the selling tools.

Checklist No. 9
Motivating the Sales Force to Superior Performance

TOPIC	OK	NEEDS SOME WORK	KEY AREA FOR ATTEN-TION	DOES NOT APPLY

Compensation

1. A salary or guaranteed income plan is in effect and is attracting the type of sales force we want.

2. Several kinds of contingent compensation have been studied, and a package that is good for the company and good for the salesman has been developed and implemented.

3. All our compensation arrangements are clear to the man, measurable by him, and based on facts rather than subjective ratings or discretionary allocations.

4. Our sales force feels that it is paid adequately and promptly and that any changes will be a matter of mutual agreement.

5. Our compensation plan is consistent with company objectives. It incites the salesman to do those things that are best for the company.

6. Each salesman and supervisor has an individual standard of performance; he has helped develop it and is committed to attaining it.

7. The benefit program is tailored to the special needs of a sales force, and we use it to attract and hold good men.

8. Supplemental benefits in the way of privileges or perquisites are appropriate for the job, awarded fairly, and are an effective motivating force.

Checklist No. 9
(Continued)

TOPIC	OK	NEEDS SOME WORK	KEY AREA FOR ATTEN- TION	DOES NOT APPLY
9. Increases in compensation are tied to individual performance and are not based on group or anniversary factors.	____	____	____	____

Incentives and Contests

10. We have an effective program of company-wide and local incentives and contests.	____	____	____	____
11. They are designed for our special needs and emphasize brevity, fairness, and prompt reward.	____	____	____	____
12. They are not a substitute for a sound compensation package or an attempt to disguise another problem.	____	____	____	____
13. There is effective recognition of individual and unit accomplishment through special awards or publicity.	____	____	____	____
14. We do not create motivational problems by criticizing performance publicly.	____	____	____	____

Career Development

15. The value of career development and the costs of high turnover are recognized. We do keep our best men.	____	____	____	____
16. The promotion requirements for the future have been calculated, and we have attracted the right-size group of promotable men.	____	____	____	____
17. Our men have been told of the opportunities available and are being given special training and testing.	____	____	____	____

18. Our compensation package has

Checklist No. 9
(Continued)

TOPIC	OK	NEEDS SOME WORK	KEY AREA FOR ATTEN-TION	DOES NOT APPLY
been tailored to hold on to those men who can assume additional responsibility.	___	___	___	___
19. A realistic program of parallel development gives field salesmen a chance to grow and still remain in the territory.	___	___	___	___
20. We are able to retain those field salesmen we want, and their performance indicates that they are properly motivated.	___	___	___	___

Summary

21. Each salesman and supervisor knows what his complete compensation, benefits, and incentive program is.	___	___	___	___
22. He can calculate his own earnings exactly based on information available to him promptly and regularly.	___	___	___	___
23. He has agreed to a specific program to give him new skills or improve existing ones.	___	___	___	___
24. He knows what the company thinks of his level of performance and what future opportunities will result from continued good performance.	___	___	___	___

10 / Designing the Merchandising Program

ONE of the strengths of a market-oriented company is the way it coordinates all its contacts with customers and prospects, and unifies its merchandising effort so that one basic message comes through loud and clear. When the 11 elements in a marketing plan were analyzed in Chapter 1, the discussion of three points was deferred. Those three sections were No. 5, the merchandising program; No. 6, the field sales coverage; and No. 7, the field selling program. The preceding chapters have dealt with the organization and staffing of the field sales force. Now it is time to create the selling programs that will give the field force its voice. The message carried by the salesman must blend harmoniously with all the other communications the company is sending out. Thus the initial step in developing the selling program to be used in the field is to define the complete company merchandising effort. The overall goal is to reach the decision makers and to help them move through the steps of a purchase.

Attaining the goal depends on careful analysis of the campaign's two major elements, the demand side and the supply side. The *demand* side is concerned with the customer or prospect. It identifies the people who will buy the product or service, and describes their decision-making patterns, their information needs, and their buying motives and most likely objections. The *supply* side deals with the company's response to the demand. It allocates communication responsibility among the sales force, the advertising department, and the technical and distribution groups — defining what will be said or done and who will do it. Exhibit 20 illustrates a systematic approach to spelling out the demand and supply sides of a merchandising campaign.

Many demand factors have already been pinpointed because the whole process of product development has been based on the same demand-supply concept. Therefore a great deal is already known about the people who will make the purchase, what they are looking for, and what they do not want. On the supply side, there may be opportunities to consolidate some company activities. Many selling tools are available, including direct spoken communication via the sales call, advertising in all its forms, and distribution techniques that increase the ease with which the purchase can be made.

Sometimes it is necessary to develop a separate program for each market segment; selling refrigerators to Eskimos would call for a different merchandising approach than that used to market coal in Newcastle. More often, though, some categories can be combined. For a given product the basic buying motives may be the same whether the customer is in New York, Phoenix, or Bangkok. If a company sells to wholesalers and retailers, the necessary cooperative advertising plan and in-store support are probably about the same for many of its products, regardless of location. Thus it may be possible to combine some of the features of the second component of the merchandising program — the supply side.

Coordination. Effective integration of all the aspects of merchandising, plus coordination with the production department, increases cumulative impact and avoids waste effort. The timing of each activity can be related to all others so that the sales force is not selling a product that cannot be delivered, or seeking tie-in support for an ad campaign that has already started to appear. The product catalog or brochure must emphasize the same selling arguments that the man in the field is being trained to use in his presentation. Poor coordination, an all too common problem, usually is the result of a lack of market orientation. The company is still

Exhibit 20. Developing the demand and supply sides of a merchandising campaign.

The Demand Side	The Supply Side
1. Who are the decision makers? 　a. Key 　b. Supporting 　c. Continuing	1. Who will communicate with each decision maker? 　a. Sales force 　b. Distributor or dealer 　c. Advertising or promotion 　d. Company executives 　e. Company technical group 　f. Other
2. What is the buyer's decision-making pattern? 　a. Initial purchase 　b. Repeat purchase	2. How does our planned sales coverage conform to the buyer's decision-making pattern?
3. What information is needed to advance through the steps of a purchase? 　a. Attention 　b. Interest 　c. Comparison 　d. Conviction 　e. Action	3. What information will we furnish so that we can secure: 　a. Attention 　b. Interest 　c. Comparison 　d. Conviction 　e. Action
4. What needs must be filled? What are the principal buying motives? 　a. Desire for gain 　b. Desire for improvement 　c. Desire to excel 　d. Desire for recognition	4. What appeals will be made to the principal buying motives? 　a. Desire for gain 　b. Desire for improvement 　c. Desire to excel 　d. Desire for recognition
5. What are the most likely objections? 　a. Value 　b. Suitability 　c. Timing 　d. Need to consult others 　e. Personal considerations	5. What answers will we give to the prospect's objections about: 　a. Value 　b. Suitability 　c. Timing 　d. Need to consult others 　e. Personal considerations

Exhibit 20. (Continued.)

The Demand Side	The Supply Side
6. How would the buyer prefer to get delivery of his order?	6. How will we deliver the order to the buyer?
7. What after-sale needs does the customer have? a. Training b. Service c. Warranty d. Other	7. How will we supply the after-sale requirements? a. Training b. Service c. Warranty d. Other

divided into noncommunicating departments, each of them planning what it will do, not what it wants to make the customer do.

Establishing the Demand Side

The Decision Makers

The first step in clarifying the demand side is to determine who the decision makers are, and what roles they play. The person who has a need to be filled and also the authority or financial means to make a buying commitment is the central figure: the key decision maker. A purchasing agent often fits that description, but for some very important undertakings he may assume a secondary role, with the final selection being made by a senior company official. Salesmen often identify the wrong person as the key decision maker, assuming that the person looking for information is the one who will do the buying. After wasting precious hours, they find that the key decision maker is someone else.

Supporting decision makers fall into three major categories: technical, financial, and operating. The architect, consultant, or the company testing department are examples of technical decision makers, who judge the merits of what is being offered against the needs that must be filled. Financial decision makers evaluate the prospective purchase either in absolute terms, as for a large building contract, or from a value analysis viewpoint, where they put numbers next to the technical findings and compare the relative ability of two or more products or services to fill the purchaser's needs. Operating decision makers participate in the buying process by deciding on how well the purchase will work out in use, and how compatible it will be with other materials or activities.

All the important decision makers must be identified if an effective merchandising program is to be developed. It does no good to speak to the key decision maker at the executive level if those he will turn to for counsel are being ignored. Just as strongly, there is little point in a sales campaign that emphasizes only technical data and fails to communicate with the key men.

Continuing decision makers have a great deal of control over repeat purchases. They are often the same ones who participated in the initial buying decision, but now they are checking the merits of the product against the claims made for it and evaluating the actual performance to see if it meets the standards that were set. A sound merchandising campaign recognizes that there are no steady customers; there are only prospects. Every buyer always compares the merits of making a repeat purchase with the advantages of taking some other action, and he must be helped through the conviction and action steps of his purchase.

Market segments must be carefully analyzed for different categories of decision makers. For example, the sale of appliances sets up several demand components. The distributor or dealer who will carry the line is a decision-making unit. The salesmen on the retail floor constitute another, as they decide which of the several product lines they will promote. And, of course, the consumer is another decision-making center, and a difficult one to analyze.

Decision-making Patterns

Because the buying decision is often a complex one, the need to communicate with the prospect in logical sequence and in effective language calls for careful study of the customer's decision-making pattern. Sometimes only one decision maker is involved, and he moves through the steps of a purchase rapidly; buying a newspaper that carries an arresting headline is an example. At the other extreme, a contractor's decision to standardize on one line of earth-moving equipment could take months and would call for the opinions of many technical, financial, and operating decision makers.

The sales manager needs to be sure that his company thoroughly understands the decision-making patterns of his customers. One good way to do this is to put the sequence on paper, as shown in Exhibit 21. The original equipment manufacturer analyzed in the example has a definite routine to be followed whenever a new source is being considered for any component. It is evident that the

Exhibit 21. A manufacturer's decision-making pattern for selecting a new source for components.

Function	Individual or Group	Activity
Secure information about new sources	Purchasing agent	Asks for samples, prices, and specifications.
Performance test	Engineering manager	Tests samples in laboratory, reports results, and makes recommendation.
Value analysis	Purchasing department	Compares new source with present one and makes recommendation.
Authorization for trial order	Vice-president, manufacturing	Acts on engineering and purchasing recommendations.
Production efficiency	Production manager	Uses trial lot in regular production and reports on suitability.
Performance evaluation	Engineering manager	Tests complete units incorporating component from new source, and makes recommendation.
Customer satisfaction	Sales manager	Analyzes effect of new component on sales and makes recommendation.
Recommendation to purchase in quantity	Purchasing agent	Assembles all reports, proposes action, secures concurrence of other supporting decision makers.
Decision to purchase in quantity	Vice-president, manufacturing	Accepts recommendation and authorizes issuance of purchase order.

vice-president of manufacturing is the key decision maker, and that the managers of purchasing, engineering, production, and sales are in supporting roles. Charts that clearly portray the customer's pattern should be part of any company's marketing plan. They make sure that all agree on who is involved in the buying decision, and therefore on whom the merchandising program must talk to.

The Steps in a Purchase

Every purchase follows the same orderly sequence of development, progressing initially from attention to interest, then to comparison of alternatives, leading to a conviction about the best solution for the purchaser's need, and finally to action that puts the solution into effect. The marketing plan must identify the information needed by each type of decision maker as he or she moves through each step of the purchase. When these demand components have been defined, it will be easier to create the merchandising materials and to take the physical actions that will communicate to the buyer what he must know before he can make a favorable decision.

Attention. The purchaser must know that the product exists, his attention should be drawn to it in a positive way that creates a good impression, and he must form the opinion that the product might fill a need that he has. This is why, for example, fruit and vegetable merchants put so much emphasis on the presentation or packaging of what has been grown; they know they must get the prospect's attention by creating images of attractiveness, freshness, and good flavor or nutrition.

Interest. Once his attention has been gained, the buyer then decides whether he is interested in learning more. He must be able to find out enough about features, availability, and cost to satisfy himself that careful consideration of a purchase would be to his advantage. The couple looking for a chair for the den may have their attention drawn to an attractive sample on the dealer's floor. Immediate delivery will help them become interested; being told that it must be ordered from the factory, with a 12-week delay, may just as surely make them swing their attention to another chair.

Comparison. When the purchaser has moved to this third step, he is seriously considering making a favorable decision. He needs to get specific answers to all his questions and to have all the data that will enable him to compare one product with another, or with a different way of spending his money. He is now eliminating alternatives, and is considering the timing and quantity of his purchase and the price he will pay.

Conviction. When the fourth step is reached, the decision-making process is approaching a conclusion. Having studied all the aspects that interest him, the buyer is ready to make up his mind. Sometimes the assent is a passive one, as with the cafeteria customer who looks down the line to see what others are ordering and decides to have the roast beef because it's so popular. The conviction may take the form of a counterproposal, as when a buyer offers his idea of the correct price for a piece of real estate. In a well-organized business, conviction is the result of careful study, but it can often be speeded up if the seller knows whom to talk to and what to say.

Action. The final step in a purchase is the commitment to buy — the ultimate goal of the company's merchandising program. But this will come about only if the needs of all the decision makers have been filled through the whole purchasing sequence. The prospect may appear to be indecisive, but the fault may not be with him so much as with the information that has been supplied to him and his associates by the seller.

Identifying Buying Motives

There must be agreement within the company about the buying motives of its customers and prospects. The market-oriented company has dedicated itself to filling needs; it responds to demands, and those demands must be clearly understood if the supply side of the merchandising program is to have the desired impact on the buying public.

The interplay of buying motives is a fascinating area of study. Two people may buy the same product to fill entirely different needs, one stressing utility and the other beauty. The same product can answer many demands within a complex decision-making group. New furniture for the offices may satisfy the president's need to have the business appear successful; the personnel manager's need for modern, comfortable working conditions that attract better employees; and the office manager's need to fit more people into the same space by using coordinated modular equipment. In defining the demand side of its merchandising program, a company will find that customers' buying motives usually fall into one of four categories.

Desire for gain. The basic buying appeal is either money or the effect of money. A business may make a purchase because it can make a profit through resale or because it can reduce its operating costs. Many buyers are interested in saving time, which they equate with money, or in benefiting from the experience of others, which they consider as eliminating the need to spend time and money on investigation. While many purchases do not involve a desire for gain, no merchandising program is complete unless it has carefully looked for opportunities to fill the widespread desire to profit from one's actions.

Desire for improvement. How many times have we said, "There must be a better way to do this!" That plea puts in words the second of the key buying motives, the desire for improvement. People want to know if a favorable buying decision means that a task is simplified or made safer. They want to increase their efficiency or improve their health. The goal is to find that life is happier, easier, or more secure because the purchase filled a need better than it had been filled before.

Desire to excel. In the preceding chapters a great deal of emphasis has been placed on the salesman's need to know "what constitutes doing a good job." This same urge is present in all people as the need to excel, to obtain a feeling of accomplishment. When considering a purchase, the buyer wants to know what it will do for his self-esteem. Will he be the first to have the product, or will he have the best one that is made? Will it help him do his job better than he could without it? Competition — whether athletic, business, or social — is a powerful motivating force, and the demand for ways to compete better will not abate.

Desire for recognition. Many purchases fill the buyer's need for the approval of others. In its direct form, it means being influenced by what others think or by the need to associate with success. A successful new fashion in clothing is often the expression of many people's desire to look like the leaders who launched the styles. The desire for recognition can also be an indirect buying motive, as when a technical decision maker will have as his basic interest the need to be thought of as efficient and knowledgeable. The company that helps him look good will often be the one whose product he recommends.

Defining the Most Likely Objections

A buyer's objection is one of the clearest demand components in the building of a merchandising program. The seller has been trying to move the prospect along the steps of a purchase, but now he has met with opposition. The constructive view of an objection is that it is really a request for more information, not an evasion or an excuse. Accurate identification of those objections most likely to impede the progress toward a sale helps to increase the realism of the whole merchandising approach. If what is being said does not answer the buyer's legitimate questions and doubts, it may end up as a pretty advertisement or a spectacular sales call, and the sale will be lost. Most objections can be classified under five major headings.

Value. Just as the desire for gain is the strongest buying motive, the fear of loss is the strongest argument against making a purchase. If the customer does not believe that the proposed product or service offers good value, he will reject it at the comparison step, and his conviction will be to decide against buying. Doubts about value can include such areas as price, terms of sale, trade discount, trade-in, or lack of difference when compared with what the buyer is presently using.

Suitability. This is one of the favorite objections of those in supporting roles in the decision-making process. The design or performance may not be just right, or the product may be considered too new and too risky. Perhaps it will not meet the buyer's standards for quality, and be thought of as too expensive or too cheap to fill the customer's need. Objections based on suitability can often be answered in advance if the sales and merchandising programs are properly structured.

Timing. Just as the market-oriented company has a realistic plan and timetable for its operations, so do its customers — even though the customer may have his plan only in his mind and not on paper. He wants his need filled by a certain time and wants to pay for his purchase according to his own financial ideas. The merchandising program must convince him that action now will be to his interest, and that further delay may only aggravate the problem that he is trying to solve.

Need to consult others. What the seller sees as a delay in moving through the steps of a purchase is nothing more than taking time for systematic analysis, in the mind of the buyer. Whatever the field, the decision maker may need to seek the counsel of his superiors or the advice of his supporting associates, who are studying details of the proposed move. Buying committees, or co-signatures from someone in authority, are a frequently used method of insuring that purchases meet the buyer's standards. A sound merchandising plan provides answers to those who must have facts and figures before they can make the decision.

Knowledge of the customer's decision-making pattern also makes it easier to fill his information demands in logical sequence, and not ruin the chances of a sale by trying to fight or ignore the established procedure.

Personal considerations. The sales force sector deals more with objections that involve personal considerations than do the broader aspects of merchandising. A television advertisement cannot discuss all the possible combinations of color and design available in an automobile, although it can and should emphasize those that have the broadest appeal. Personal objections are frequently among the last to be voiced, but often the most important.

Delivering the Order

An essential ingredient of a complete merchandising program is the analysis of how the customer would prefer to take delivery of his order. Efficient distribution is just as much a response to demand as is creative advertising; the customer, not the company, should be the controlling factor. Failure to satisfy his needs may mean the loss of a sale at an early stage; "occupancy late next year" may deter a businessman from even inspecting an office building under construction. Mistakes in delivery can frustrate efforts to obtain a repeat order; every salesman can cite many such instances.

Careful study will identify the key delivery demands. *Timing* is perhaps the most obvious one, and proper response to this need can often move the prospect to the action step; he can get what he wants when he wants it, so he makes the decision to buy.

Packaging influences all buyers, from the largest government agency to the individual housewife. Business demands, such as the need to offer 500-gram packages for export in addition to the one-pound packages sold domestically, affect sales.

Usability is a powerful motivating factor; the faster the buyer can benefit from his purchase, the better he likes it. Whether the product is a lawn mower, a numerically controlled lathe, or a convenience food, the ability to use it quickly and without trouble is always in the buyer's mind.

Other examples of delivery requirements only emphasize even more strongly that it is not enough to get the order, and that the chances of making a sale are greatly affected by the company's arrangements for storage, distribution, packaging, and customer assistance. Just as the buying motives and objections were examined (and they often include aspects of the delivery cycle), so must the precise delivery needs of the customer be tabulated. When this has been done it is easier to demonstrate to all company departments how they can help sales by modifying their practices, and by doing things the way the customer, and not necessarily the department manager, thinks they should be done.

After-Sale Demands

The public be damned philosophy is a Stone Age relic; every successful business recognizes the value of having satisfied customers. The problem comes with the definition of "satisfied," and this final section of the demand side is concerned with identifying the after-sale needs so that the buyer will order again or will speak well of his supplier to other potential customers. Careful enumeration of postsale requirements also helps promote the market-oriented concept within the company, since the response, or supply action, will have to come from many departments, not from marketing alone.

Training can mean including an informative brochure with a kitchen appliance so that the housewife can educate herself in its use. It can also mean a multimillion-dollar flight simulator that helps airlines train jumbo jet pilots. Both actions are merchandising oriented, and result from advance analysis of what the customer will need after the order has been placed.

Service is so important a factor in customer thinking that it often is the copy platform in major national advertising; "Sears services what it sells," for example.

Warranty protection is a frequent buying motive, but the customer will judge not only the promise but also the performance. What does he or she really expect? Is the analysis truly seeking to make the customer happy, or is it only trying to find out how little service the company can get away with?

Other after-sale demands include proper invoicing and handling of payments (try calling on an account that has just received an incorrect past due notice). The seller's long-term obligations can also be very important to the customer; the equipment buyer wants to be able to buy parts and supplies at a fair price for the life of the machine.

Consolidating the Demand Components

An orderly consolidation of the demand components completes the organization of the first part of the company merchandising program. Exhibit 20 illustrated how to collect all the needed information and in a way that will aid the subsequent development of the supply side. By listing the several decision makers, and the decision-making pattern used in the buying process, it will be possible to allocate selling responsibilities to the appropriate company department—whether it be the field force, the advertising department, or, in some cases, the president. Pinpointing the information needed to move the buyers through the steps of a purchase makes it easier to develop "rifle" answers—concise, full of facts, and communicated in terms the buyer understands. Knowing what buying motives and objections will be encountered aids the orderly development of selling material. If testimonials, performance reports, or government agency approval will be required, a great deal of lead time can be saved. Better to know what is needed before the selling begins than to find out after the sales team has struck out.

Finally, those developing the merchandising program must put themselves in the buyer's position and ask, "If I do place an order, what do I expect in the way of delivery and after-sale assistance?"

Once all these demand components are identified, the company can begin to create a comprehensive response. All departments, not only marketing, must contribute, and the answer must be a unified message that talks to its audience about beneficial solutions to the customer's requirements.

Creating the Supply Side

The process of developing the supply side of the merchandising program is a mirror image of the sequence used to identify the demand components. The assignments can be distributed and the final merchandising impact will be both cohesive and pertinent with the same format as used in Exhibit 20. The major responsibilities need not be allocated on an exclusive basis; careful coordination of many people's efforts will produce far better results than a policy of "let the sales force handle the selling job and everybody else keep their hands off." The market segments in which the company operates must clearly be the basis for deciding who is to do what, and how.

Communicating with the decision makers. In marketing grocery products, the consumer's demands for information are usually allocated to the advertising and promotion group. The need is to reach a very large number of people with an uncomplicated message, with mass media coverage being the best answer. The field sales force, at the same time, will be charged with the responsibility of supplying the information needs of the wholesale and retail trade, giving them the details of pricing, delivery, special deals, timing of promotions, and other facts the buyer needs to maximize his sales and profits.

A far different situation can be true in merchandising capital goods. The entire function of direct communication may be assigned to the territory manager, except for a limited advertising program in trade publications. True, there will be brochures and technical publications, but they are designed to help him communicate with prospects and not to be a direct message in themselves.

Conforming to the decision-making pattern. Once the customer's pattern for arriving at a buying decision has been defined, the development of imaginative selling responses becomes easier, although not easy. Sometimes the decision is that one man should make practically all the contacts with every one of the decision makers. As an example, each salesman for a very large wholesaler would have his assigned accounts, and he alone would see the buyer or owner, the shop assistants or storekeepers, as well as handle complaints and administrative questions.

The manufacturer's decision-making pattern in Exhibit 21 would demand a different response. Although the territory manager would have the central communication responsibility, he could be aided by other company employees who had either the expert knowledge, personal acquaintance, or official title to make their participation desirable. One approach could look like the accompanying chart:

Decision Maker in Buyer's Organization	Persons in Seller's Organization Responsible for Communication
Vice-president, manufacturing	Regional manager, aided by territory manager
Purchasing agent	Territory manager
Engineering manager	Manager, technical services, aided by territory manager
Production manager	Territory manager
Sales manager	Regional manager, aided by territory manager
Value analysis group in purchasing department	Territory manager, aided by accounting manager and manager, technical services

The critical consideration, of course, is that the supply responsibility be assigned to the person or unit most knowledgeable and best qualified to give the customer the information he needs. This enlightened approach to merchandising in the market-oriented company can be quite different from that of the conventional or departmental type of organization. With market orientation, everybody is a marketing man, and every marketing man is a merchandiser. By using the talents of all his employees, the seller can match the decision-making pattern of the buyer to those in his company who, regardless of title, can best help the progress through the steps of a purchase.

The steps in a sale. The demand side of the merchandising campaign has listed the information that the customer needs to move through the five steps of a purchase. When the responses are developed, they become the company's plan to move through the same sequence; its actions become the steps in a sale. Having decided what is required, the merchandising group must now supply it in a way that makes something happen. It was many years ago when the customer asked the difference between two models of a kitchen appliance and was told "eight dollars," but the story still has plenty of meaning. It is not enough to answer a customer's request for information; the answer must cause a favorable action.

Responding to buying motives and objections. The amount and kind of information to be supplied to customers and prospects is an area where many companies waste great amounts of time and money through poor definition of needs and responses. How many display kits have been prepared without adequate definition of what is to be said, where they are to be used, and how much space is available in the customer's location? How many "executive visits" have produced a negative rather than a positive effect because not enough preparatory time was spent determining which decision makers would be seen, what they wanted to know, and what they would be told?

Effective merchandising comes about from a coordinated response to information needs, buying motives, and objections. If the aim is to secure attention and interest, the instinctive reaction is to produce colorful, heavily illustrated material with brief copy, which will command attention when mailed or delivered on the call. The buyer looking for technical data will throw the material away. If the key buying motive is absolute reliability of performance, a brochure emphasizing the exotic materials used in manufacturing or featuring attractive models partially obscuring the product constitutes poor merchandising. So, too, would be a sales presentation that emphasized reliability of performance, but under conditions that the prospect would consider as "different" from his business.

The timing is just as important as the content, and this is another value of the coordinated marketing plan. When they have expert knowledge, as with technical products, the salesmen should have the opportunity to comment on the advertising and sales promotion plan. Mistakes such as choosing the wrong magazines, advertising during the wrong months, and, even worse, saying the wrong things can often be avoided. By the same token, it is not preaching heresy to advocate that those who are expert in market analysis should examine the lists of customers and prospects and agree with the sales coverage plan that has been developed.

Delivery and after-sale responsibilities. Hardly a sales meeting goes by without someone saying, "A sale is not complete until the goods are paid for," and it's true. It is just as true that the sale is not complete "until the customer is satisfied that he's satisfied." When the demand side was developed, the delivery and after-sale functions were listed. If the customer is to be just as happy with his purchase as the producer or merchant is with his sale, these functions must be performed. The field sales manager will want to be sure that the best man or unit has been assigned to each function; that the equipment, procedure, or technique is the best that can be devised; and that the goal of everyone is to pave the way to another sale.

Summary

An integrated merchandising program will greatly increase the on-the-call effectiveness of the field sales force; and no marketing plan is complete until there is complete agreement on content, timing, and responsibility. Before developing the specific selling aids and sales programs to be used by his territory managers, the field sales manager will want to be sure that his company has properly organized the vital merchandising function; the following checklist will help him make that judgment.

Checklist No. 10
Designing the Merchandising Program

TOPIC	OK	NEEDS SOME WORK	KEY AREA FOR ATTEN- TION	DOES NOT APPLY

Coordinating the Program

1. Our merchandising effort is the result of systematic analysis of the demand side and the supply side. It is a scientific, as well as an artistic, program. ___ ___ ___ ___

2. The timing and coordination of all merchandising activities, and their integration with production schedules, is excellent. ___ ___ ___ ___

3. The content of our communications is consistent throughout. We tell the same story to the same customer or prospect, whether on the call, in print, or through other media. ___ ___ ___ ___

Establishing the Demand Side

4. The key decision makers in our major customer and prospect categories have been identified. ___ ___ ___ ___

5. We have also pinpointed the type of people who act as supporting or continuing decision makers. ___ ___ ___ ___

6. For each market segment, we understand the decision-making pattern that the customer follows, and have prepared charts that show the flow and the people involved. ___ ___ ___ ___

7. Each decision maker needs certain information to proceed through the five steps of a purchase. We know what information he needs. ___ ___ ___ ___

8. The principal buying motives of each

Checklist No. 10
(Continued)

TOPIC	OK	NEEDS SOME WORK	KEY AREA FOR ATTEN- TION	DOES NOT APPLY
decision maker have been identified, and we understand what incites him to action.	⎯⎯	⎯⎯	⎯⎯	⎯⎯
9. The most likely objections have been established, and we know what questions the decision makers are apt to raise.	⎯⎯	⎯⎯	⎯⎯	⎯⎯
10. The customer's needs as far as the delivery of the order and the form in which it comes to him have been tabulated.	⎯⎯	⎯⎯	⎯⎯	⎯⎯
11. The after-sale requirements that help to make for satisfied customers have been defined.	⎯⎯	⎯⎯	⎯⎯	⎯⎯
12. All the above demand components have been consolidated (see Exhibit 20 for one way to do it), and we have a clear picture of whom we must talk to, what information is wanted, and how a purchase is made.	⎯⎯	⎯⎯	⎯⎯	⎯⎯

Creating the Supply Side

13. The responsibility for communicating with the decision makers has been allocated. Advertising, promotion, field sales, and other merchandising groups each know what functions are to be performed.	⎯⎯	⎯⎯	⎯⎯	⎯⎯
14. Our efforts conform to the customer's decision-making pattern. We send the right men, in the right sequence, regardless of where they come from in our company.	⎯⎯	⎯⎯	⎯⎯	⎯⎯

Checklist No. 10
(Continued)

TOPIC	OK	NEEDS SOME WORK	KEY AREA FOR ATTEN-TION	DOES NOT APPLY
15. Our merchandising activities are designed to move prospects logically through each step of the sale.	___	___	___	___
16. The best appeals to buying motives have been devised, and are communicated clearly to those decision makers who are seeking information.	___	___	___	___
17. Effective ways of handling objections have been developed, and customers are satisfied with the answers they receive.	___	___	___	___
18. Delivery and after-sale responsibilities are well taken care of. We do everything necessary to insure customer goodwill and to earn repeat orders.	___	___	___	___
19. The sales force has been consulted about our media schedules, where applicable, and there is complete coordination and mutual support between field sales and advertising.	___	___	___	___

11 / Providing the Selling Tools

THE mission of the sales force is to make successful sales calls. Period. If its mission were anything else, the company would have been better off hiring statisticians or servicemen or analysts. The sales call is the central supply action of the field sales team; it responds to the needs of customer and prospect for information and assistance in making a purchase. Informative and imaginative selling tools make good calls better—the goal of Step 2 in Phase 4. The sequence of development includes these five actions:

- Definition of the principal types of sales calls that will be made
- Analysis of the eight components of a complete sales call to determine the selling goals that must be attained
- Identification of the selling aids and sales programs needed
- Their design and field testing
- Instruction in their use

Defining the Principal Types of Sales Calls

A sales call is most successful when it strikes a balance between opposing forces. It must be carefully planned and executed, but it cannot be a sequence of go or no-go mechanical actions and re-actions. It should follow certain rules and pursue a logical path; yet the prospect must never feel that he is getting a canned presentation. It must be a scientific exercise, using tested selling principles.

However there is an art to selling that calls for an individual style, a way of acting and talking that builds warm personal communication. Many things must be blended, and the sales manager who defines the kinds of calls his men make can help them increase their success ratio by providing them with selling programs that encourage rather than restrict the personal factor. Even though every sales call is an individual and special effort, most companies find that their sales force's activities can be classified into relatively few major categories.

Program presentation. The major sales call that establishes the basic buyer-seller relationship can be called the program presentation. If a company is launching an important new product into the consumer field, it will need a carefully developed sales presentation for its wholesalers and retailers. The salesman must explain the features and profit potential of the new product, secure initial orders, and arrange for a joint merchandising program to create local consumer demand. It is no easy task, and certainly not one that can be turned over to him without a complete package of the sales aids he needs.

Similarly, a proposed purchase of expensive capital equipment usually reaches the stage where the initial testing and determination of customer need have been completed. The manufacturer must now make a complete proposal covering recommended models, number of units, price, delivery, warranty, training, and service. His territory manager should be provided with an imaginative and organized way of getting this story across clearly and affirmatively. Just about any business needs a program presentation as a basic selling tool for its sales force.

Planned sales coverage. Guidelines for the frequency with which accounts are to be seen have already been established; and now the selling problem is, "What do you do with an account you call on every two weeks (or months)?" If the answer is to just keep calling and looking for business, the company and the salesman have surrendered the initiative; that is, the customer will control the interview. Repeat business is earned only by moving the customer once again through the final steps of a purchase, and the salesman must have material that reinforces the wisdom of the original buying decision and that makes it easy for the account to buy again.

If the account is still only a prospect, the salesman must be able to gain attention and start the progress toward the initial order. Must he rely solely on his own voice, or will the company supply him with creative sales aids that speed the conversion from prospect to customer?

Training and merchandising assistance. It could well be that the after-sale activities are as important as the sale itself. The last order must be moved off the shelf before the retailer will buy again. If an industrial machine has been sold, neglect of the user will almost guarantee that there will be no future orders. The market-oriented company has a great advantage here, because there is a free flow of information among departments. The service and technical information and aids that the salesman needs are developed jointly by sales and engineering. The entire merchandising team, including company associates and outside agencies, pitches in to make him an effective local advertising expert, skilled in selling through his customers, not merely to them.

Troubleshooting. Dealing with a customer complaint usually means the temporary loss of the dominant position. The salesman is not calling on the account, but rather it is the account that has demanded his presence. If the marketing plan has been properly developed, the man in the field knows what his duties are and how much authority he has. But what selling aids have been developed to change a complaint into a sales benefit? How can the salesman reassure the customer? Analysis of the demand side has answered the question, "If I were the customer, what would I need to convince me that I am being treated fairly?" Attention must now be turned to giving the salesman the selling tools he will use to handle complaints in a positive way.

Special sales activities. All businesses are different in some way from each other, and examination of the differences should include a clear definition of all the major types of sales calls. Granted that the man in the territory makes program presentations and the other kinds of calls listed above. What else does he do; how can it be described? What is he trying to get the customer to do? What information does the prospect want? How can the company help the salesman present his case quickly, clearly, and with success?

Analysis of the Eight Components of a Sales Call

Each individual sales call should be a complete event, a systematic linking of several actions to produce a specific result. Certainly the success factor in selling is due in large part to the salesman's ability and skill, but it also depends on the effectiveness of the materials he works with. In providing tools to his men, the sales manager should review each type of sales call they make, and ask himself what can be supplied for each of the eight components of a complete sales call: planning, approach, presentation, handling objections, accomplishing the objective, call-back foundation, postcall analysis, and recording.

Planning. The first component of a call is advance planning. The salesman must identify the decision maker he is to see, determine where that person stands in the progress through the steps of a purchase, and what information will interest him. Adequate territory sales records should provide him with answers for both his customers and his prospects. Next comes the selection of the objective of the sales call—the reason why the salesman is there. When this is decided, the most effective kind of presentation can be chosen, and the correct selling materials can be organized for easy use during the call. Planning guides should be supplied to help the salesman organize himself.

Approach. The sales call must begin with some action that makes the buyer want to hear more. In calling on prospects, the salesman needs material that identifies both himself and his company, and in a way that will interest the listener. For planned sales coverage, he needs a steady stream of new material from his company, so that he can open each call with a refreshing new note instead of "Well, here I am again."

Presentation. Five main types of sales presentations will answer the needs of most salesmen. For a *proposal,* they need pictures, specification sheets, comparative data, and covers or binders. The recommendation must be attractively packaged, and it must impress the buyer with its thoroughness. To make an effective *demon-*

stration, the need can range all the way from a hand-held sample box to the organization of a complex machinery field day. *Testimonials* make effective presentations if the buyer can identify himself with the situation. Office equipment companies, as an example, have done outstanding work in providing their salesmen with documented stories of product use in many fields. More and more a sales presentation revolves around *audiovisual material,* clearly management's responsibility to design, test, and then furnish to the field force. Many orders, both initial and repeat, are won by a *response,* when the salesman returns with the answer to a problem or a question. He needs the same types of tools as he did for a proposal so that the buyer knows that serious attention has been given to his request for more information.

Handling objections. Within an individual market segment, objections by the buyer can frequently be anticipated, and the sales call must include satisfactory answers. Sometimes an objection will be handled during the presentation, but often the salesman will wait to see if the buyer raises it. The company must give its field men authoritative answers that obviously carry the backing of the corporation and are not viewed by the prospect as sales talk.

Accomplishing the objective. Not every sales call has as its objective getting an immediate order, but it does have a specific selling purpose. How can the company help its men attain their objectives? What sales aids will make the buyer say yes, or gain the support of a technical man or a purchasing analyst? How can a key decision maker be convinced that his account is being properly handled so that he gives a repeat order?

Call-back foundation. Where there is to be another call, the salesman can maintain his strong position if he can define in advance (1) the date of the call, (2) who will be seen, (3) for what purpose, and (4) what must be done before the next meeting. The company must help the salesman become an "insider" in the customer's eyes, one who is helping rather than merely selling. It does so by designing material that helps him establish the right foundation for the next call.

Postcall analysis. Did the call reach its objective? If not, what lessons can be learned? Were the selling materials effective, or should they be changed? The man in the field must be encouraged to ask for changes in the tools he works with, and also urged to develop his own local sales aids.

Recording. This final step in a sales call is also part of the first step in the next call on the same account. Has the salesman been given efficient equipment to record the sales activity in his territory? Is he required to fill out lengthy additional reports for his supervisor? If the territory becomes vacant, does the company know what went on, and can a new man start with a full bank of data about customers and prospects?

Identifying the Selling Aids and Sales Programs Needed

Accurate definition of the demand side and of the salesman's sales call activities has greatly improved the chances of developing a superior package of selling aids and sales programs. Most material furnished to the sales force can be classified under one of three categories: basic equipment, individual territory aids, or special material for individual market segments.

Basic Selling Equipment

The first priority is to equip the salesman with a selling package that will help him to do more business with present customers and to bring in initial orders from new accounts. The most important items include:

Information about the company. What will convince the buyer that he is dealing with a responsible supplier? What will help to strengthen the bonds with present customers?

Product selling aids. There must be a unified package of complete, up-to-date, and customer-oriented data about the company's products. The one-item buyer does not want a 150-page general line catalog, whereas the purchasing agent needs more than an ad reprint. Samples, brochures, pictures, all sorts of visual aids can be developed to help the salesman tell his product story.

Prices and terms of sale. Just as the sales manager needs a clear statement about pricing, so does the man in the territory. He must be equipped to give the customer prompt and accurate quotations or to get the facts needed for a speedy response.

Information about company services. Buyers are more impressed with written material that they can keep than they are with salesmen's words. If the company offers delivery, service, or warranty arrangements, they need to be presented clearly and attractively.

Order books and territory records. The company wants each man to be a successful territory manager. It must provide him with the record systems and planning guides he needs for effective direction of his selling effort, and of course with an efficient way of channeling orders back to the office or factory.

Individual Territory Aids

The basic selling equipment used throughout the sales team must now be personalized to fit the information needs, buying motives, and objections of the accounts in each individual sales territory. Many companies leave this up to the salesman completely, thereby losing an opportunity to develop effective sales aids at a very low cost. The range of territorial equipment is broad, but a few examples will indicate what can be done.

Presentation folders. If each man is given a high-quality binder with removable transparent pages, he is encouraged to develop his own local material. The product catalog may tell its story very well, but a local testimonial increases the impact. Pictures of satisfied customers, reports from testing agencies, or examples of effective local advertisements can help to win sales. Furnishing the salesman with the best in presentation folders (or authorizing him to buy one) is money well spent.

Cameras and recorders. The value of a camera in creating personalized selling aids has been demonstrated time and again. Tape recorders may also have merit, although it is usually harder to get effective material on tape than in a picture.

Audiovisual material. If the salesman is creative enough to develop his own programs, it's a wise investment to furnish him with a slide projector and to let him know which other territory managers can exchange their ideas and material with his.

Local information. When advertising rates, freight costs, or delivery methods are of local importance, the salesman should be encouraged to spend the few dollars necessary to have made maps, tables, or charts that present the information in the way the customer wants. Scrawled notes, or a lengthy schedule full of unimportant data, do not make the buyer feel that he is getting personal attention.

Special Material for Individual Market Segments

The concept of individual market segments is a central theme in the company's entire marketing effort. Product development, for example, is a planned sequence of identifying needs and supplying solutions. The selling program needs the same precision, and the territory manager must have material that is tuned to the special requirements of his customers.

User benefit information. Most products or services can be sold to a number of people with varying needs and interests. The individual buyer wants to know what the product will do for him alone. If there are many identical buyers, a four-color brochure may be the ideal selling tool, but a single typed page can be just as meaningful if it speaks directly to the purchaser.

Having decided what types and classes of customers it will call on, the company must take the shotgun material it has developed as basic selling tools and narrow its focus. Selling forklift trucks is a broad category, and general catalogs can do an effective job of presenting the full line and the company's service capability. To sell a lift truck for use in a furniture warehouse is a specialized application, and the specific user benefits must be accurately portrayed in selling aids that help to get the order.

Third-party information. Not every company fully utilizes the great amount of information issued by interested third parties, such as government testing bureaus, trade associations, and educational organizations. Professionally made motion pictures costing many thousands of dollars can often be obtained for a few hundred dollars per copy. Reports that analyze how people use a particular product, or that compare the performance of competitive products in or out of the seller's industry, can have great impact. Trends in the use of a new product can help to convince many prospects that it is time for a change, especially if some respected research group is issuing the report.

No selling campaign is complete until a thorough search has

been made for third-party information. The secretary of the trade association, the city or university librarian, or the government employee can be valuable sources of merchandising aids. Usually all it takes is a direct question, "Do you know of any material that bears on this subject (the objective of the market segment campaign)?"

Capitalizing on success. Developing selling equipment for a specialized market is sometimes a question of finding out what the best salesmen are doing, and making their tools or ideas available to all men. Handsome dividends can be earned if the company encourages its territory managers to try new approaches, monitors their progress, and rewards success. The man who is face to face with the customer makes up in motivation what he may lack in artistic or graphic skill. He may not have the prettiest selling aids, but they mean a lot to his audience.

Other Selling Equipment

A good salesman costs $20 or more per hour when the amount of time he can devote to in-person selling is compared with the total cost of maintaining him and his backup support. Wise sales managers provide the best in transportation and communication equipment to their men; they want their men selling, not driving or writing.

Automobiles. Most companies provide excellent transportation or make fair allowances when the salesman must furnish his own car. If company automobiles are supplied, it pays to set a policy about hiring a replacement car when the company vehicle needs repair. Many a selling day has been lost because the salesman feared he would be criticized for hiring a second car, a fine example of a company being penny wise and pound foolish. If the salesman receives a mileage allowance, he has an incentive against efficient coverage of his territory and is tempted to add miles as a way of making money. Either a flat monthly fee, plus actual operating expenses, or a company car is the answer.

Communications. The concept of creating maximum selling time should extend to the authorization of communication equipment. A telephone in the car or clearance to use long-distance at his discretion helps the territory manager handle crises and opportunities quickly and efficiently. An allowance for local stenographic help, or the furnishing of a typewriter and a calculator, usually returns far more in sales gained than the modest cost. If the sales manager is really trying to make his men territory managers and not territory workers, he will provide the money or the tools to eliminate clerical drudgery.

Local funds. Not often thought of as a selling aid, a local fund under the salesman's control will enable him to support his customers' activities with contributions to joint meetings or local advertisements, or by helping to pay for special services. Traditionally the company will want to have the right of advance approval, and will insist that invoices and documents be submitted before payment is made by the main or local office. If the man in the field has his own budget (and his requests will usually be modest) he becomes an on-the-spot decision maker, not an errand boy. When he writes the check himself, his customers see him as the man to deal with. If the finance department is horrified by the idea of all those men writing all those checks (a slight exaggeration), then the company is still a confederation of autonomous departments, and not a market-oriented unit.

Developing a Sales Campaign

A sales campaign is a coordinated series of actions designed to produce a cumulative effect. The goal may be to move a prospect through the five steps of a purchase, to become the exclusive supplier to a present customer, or to blunt the impact of a new competitive product. Sales campaigns represent the ultimate in field sales support, and they demonstrate the full acceptance of merchandising responsibility by the sales manager. He has already acknowledged that he must give his men the tools that will make the individual call a successful one. Now he holds himself accountable for identifying the major sales goals and for providing his men with a planned method to attain them.

In Exhibit 20 in Chapter 10 the demand and supply components of a merchandising program were listed. The development of a sales campaign follows this same sequence. Take, for example, the selling requirements of a manufacturer of mechanic's hand tools. The company knows that it must regularly provide the catalogs, the samples, the trade advertising, and all the other individual sales aids that the analysis of customer needs has defined. This year's merchandising campaign will include a major effort to win new dealers and to obtain an exclusive position with existing customers by offering a special incentive—a display board for the principal tools. Tying this board to a new order and delivery system, the company will claim that a dealer can make more profit by concentrating on one line of tools, and one line only. What should the sales manager do? He must create a series of actions that will lead the customer through all the steps of a purchase, and he must then show his men how to use this sales campaign to get orders. Exhibit 22 shows how the seven areas of demand and supply were studied and a major selling campaign created.

By deliberately analyzing all the selling tasks and selling opportunities, the sales manager has developed unusual selling tools for his men. The problem of convincing the dealer that there is adequate display space has been solved with a full-size illustration, a sample of a portion of the board, and a Polaroid camera. Work sheets, such as the profit calculator and the display installation schedule, allow the prospect to make his own comparisons, and to feel that he is being helped and not pressured. Other selling aids, including testimonials, pave the way for progress through the steps in a purchase. The man in the territory has all the assistance he needs to perform an outstanding job.

A sales campaign is developed by applying general selling principles to a specific sales task. The example shown in Exhibit 22 illustrates a simple campaign, but the concept applies even to the most complex sales problems. If the sales manager will define the major tasks his men face, he and his associates can then provide the materials and equipment needed. He works closely with brand managers and merchandising groups, but it is his responsibility to see that his men are equipped in a way that increases the tempo of their selling and that helps them make more and bigger sales.

Design and Field Testing

The many merchandising ideas must now be translated into action; it is time to design truly superior selling aids. The key to

Exhibit 22. Developing a sales campaign for an individual market segment.

Sales Objective: To secure an order for a tool display board, including opening or fill-in stock, from auto parts dealers.

The Demand Side	The Supply Side
1. Who are the decision makers?	1. Who will communicate with each decision maker?
a. *Key* Automobile parts dealer or local manager of a chain operation.	a. *Key* Territory manager.
b. *Supporting* Dealer's counter clerks. Manager's superior in central office.	b. *Supporting* Territory manager sees counter clerks. Our regional manager handles contact with central office.
c. *Continuing* Same as supporting, plus auto and truck mechanics (the dealer's customers).	c. *Continuing* Trade advertising supplements in-person calls.
2. What is the buyer's decision-making pattern?	2. What is our planned sales coverage?
a. Prospect analyzes our proposal.	a. Territory manager makes program presentation.
b. Asks counter clerks for opinion about saleability.	b. Territory manager tries to participate in discussion.
c. Checks with partners or central office for concurrence.	c. Territory manager leaves profit calculator and Polaroid picture with prospect. Regional manager will secure blanket clearance from buyer's central office.
d. Checks with mechanics and other customers on brand preferences and acceptance of our tools.	d. Trade advertising reaches some tool users. Free tools for training schools build goodwill and new user allegiance.
e. Checks with other dealers.	e. Territory manager is lining up dealers who have used program and will recommend it.

Exhibit 22. (Continued.)

The Demand Side	The Supply Side
f. Decides to buy or not buy, sets timing and amount of initial stock.	f. Territory manager tries for order after program presentation or sets definite callback date.
3. What information is needed to advance through the steps of a purchase?	3. What information will we furnish to secure:
a. *Attention* Must become aware that a new supply concept can increase his sales of handtools, at the same time reducing his inventory.	a. *Attention* Dealer knows our brand name. Use pictures of display in other dealers, plus certified profit reports.
b. *Interest* Must agree that tool display board and new supply plan are worth considering for his operation.	b. *Interest* Use foldout full-size picture to demonstrate board's compactness; show sample of board and tools; explain new reordering program (testimonials).
c. *Comparison* Needs to be able to evaluate profitability, wisdom of cutting out other lines, reliability of our promises, and acceptance by his customers.	c. *Comparison* Profit calculator lets dealer figure his return. Testimonials from other dealers prove reliability of delivery and increase in sales with one premium line properly displayed.
d. *Conviction* Must accept idea that he has room for our board, that increased profits will result, and that he will not lose business by dropping other lines.	d. *Conviction* Use Polaroid camera to show dealer holding foldout at proposed location, and get his agreement to suitability. Mechanics' brand preference survey shows our dominance in premium tool market.

Exhibit 22. (Continued.)

The Demand Side	The Supply Side
e. *Action* Must have facts about delivery, installation, price, and payment terms.	e. *Action* Display installation schedule calls for dealer to commit on time of delivery, tool assortment, and payment terms.
4. What are the most likely buying motives?	4. How will we appeal to those buying motives?
a. *Desire for gain* Profit potential from increased sales. Lower investment because of reduction in inventory.	a. *Desire for gain* Profit calculator and testimonials from dealers who used boards in test market. Express delivery plan and full line (use product line brochure) eliminate need for multiple sources.
b. *Desire for improvement* Wants store, especially counter area, to look attractive and businesslike. Reduction of pilferage and borrowing.	b. *Desire for improvement* Pictures of tool display in other dealers. Polaroid camera takes picture of proposed location with sample board in place. Special nylon retainers allow tools to be examined but not taken. No chance for shoplifting.
c. *Desire to excel* Quality products on display promote the image of being a quality source for all parts.	c. *Desire to excel* Salesman can telephone dealers who like our board and ask them to talk to prospect. Testimonials and pictures provided to salesman.
5. What are the most likely objections?	5. What answers will we give?
a. *Value* Display boards cost extra; they should be free. Tools are too high in price.	a. *Value* Boards increase sales while reducing pilferage. $50 in tool sales pays for board. Price comparison survey shows we are competitive. Brand preference survey confirms demand for our line.

Exhibit 22. (Continued.)

The Demand Side	*The Supply Side*
b. *Suitability* No space to display the board. Must order too many tools to get board. Don't sell certain types of tools.	b. *Suitability* Polaroid picture of full-size board illustration in place demonstrates board will fit. Dealer can select initial stock and has one-year exchange privilege; use testimonials.
c. *Timing* Not taking on any new lines. Too much inventory in store now.	c. *Timing* Testimonials prove that selling our line only can eliminate need to carry several lines; helps dealer cut inventory.
d. *Need to consult others* Must discuss with partners or get central office approval.	d. *Need to consult others* Profit calculator, Polaroid picture, sample of board and wrench are left with dealer. Regional manager getting central office clearance (notify men when obtained).
e. *Personal considerations* Prefer another brand of tools. Tried similar idea a few years ago and it failed.	e. *Personal considerations* Mechanics' brand preference proved by survey. "They had to show me" letters from other dealers who felt the same way but are now happy.
6. How would the buyer prefer to take delivery of his order? Wants us to install board and display tools. Wants us to inventory his stock, ship in new items, take back slow-moving numbers.	6. How will we deliver the order to the buyer? Our service man will install board (help appreciated). Telephone reorder system (we call every two weeks) insures ample, fast-moving stock.
7. What after-sale needs does the customer have?	7. How will we supply the after-sale requirements?
a. *Training* Counter clerks must know how to sell tools against low-priced competition.	a. *Training* Territory manager organizes dinner meetings, including training in sales methods.

Exhibit 22. (Continued.)

The Demand Side	The Supply Side
b. *Service* Wants low inventory, but doesn't want to be out of stock.	b. *Service* Our express delivery plan, tied to regular reorder calls, keeps the dealer in stock.
c. *Warranty* Our lifetime guarantee must not cause him expense or trouble.	c. *Warranty* Dealer orders replacements and we ship. His certification is all we need.

success is the setting of clear, customer-oriented, realistic objectives. The salesmen can expect to be well equipped, and in plenty of time, if the company will follow a few tested rules.

Establish clear objectives. A successful producer of industrial motion pictures always emphasizes the need to define the audience and the action the audience should take, and to keep the definition as narrow as possible. One of his clients, a transportation company, commissioned him to make a film about the vacation lands it served, to be shown to groups of potential travelers—a clear objective. A few weeks later he was told that the film would be shown at the annual meeting, so it should also convey the feeling that the company was profitable, well managed, and growing. Before shooting started he received additional instructions; the film would also be used in the recruiting program and would be shown to all new employees. Emphasis should therefore be placed on advancement opportunities and on individuals who had served the company well and had been equally well rewarded. The final film fell far below his standards; he even considered resigning the commission. Because it was trying to make three different audiences do three different things, the film lost all its impact, and no real message came through. Selling aids must have clear, definite, and usually single objectives.

Get expert help. The sales manager who fails to get all the expert assistance available will end up with apparently inexpensive selling aids, and they will be far less effective than they could be. He has reached the point where he can pose very direct questions and he knows exactly what he is trying to accomplish. But he is not an expert in graphics, display, or copywriting. Far better to call on the best talent in the marketing department or the advertising agency, or on local free-lancers, and let them devise the solution.

Use top-flight materials. If the customer is the most important person in the world, and he is, he deserves to be treated accordingly. Selling aids that are poorly made or that use cheap artwork or second-rate printing can be an affront to the prospect considering a purchase. A very capable advertising executive contends that the solution to the problem of high prices for selling aids is careful planning. For example, he always buys the best artwork, but he uses it several times and he knows where it will be employed before he orders the art. The quantity of selling aids is often only a guess by someone not familiar with the field sales program, as when the sales promotion manager orders 5,000 display kits without sitting down with the sales manager to agree on their use. The place to save money is in the company's own operation, not by cheapening what will go to the customer.

Field test before production. The purpose of a selling aid is not to present an idea or to communicate information. Selling aids should initiate action; they must make a prospect move through the steps of a purchase. The only way to find out if they do is by field testing them. It may not be possible to use an exact sample; after all, multicolor presses should not be used to print 10 copies. It should be possible, however, to test the concept and enough of the material to make an intelligent judgment about its effectiveness.

Some companies field test selling aids by giving them only to their best men. Wrong. All salesmen will use them, and a cross section of reactions is needed. What may be a very easy presentation for a proficient salesman may end up as a disaster in the hands of the new or average man.

Be early, not late. Proper development of a selling aid allows ample time for testing, production, and training before it will be needed. While no company will deny the truth of such a statement, few sales forces will agree that the timetable is always followed. Time after time they get their material too late, have no opportunity to become proficient in using it, and they have a valid doubt that any effective field testing was done.

Instruction in the Use of Selling Aids and Programs

Fortunately the field sales program that has already been developed has recognized the need for training, and provision has been made to teach salesmen how to use their selling aids and programs. If the material is brand new, group training is often the most effective method, especially if the attentive man approach is used to define the training objective. Individual training should supplement the group exercise, and the sales supervisor must know how to make his men skillful users of the aids the company has provided. Each new man should be given individual coaching so that he knows how to use his basic selling equipment to increase his effectiveness on the call.

Many companies believe that since most salesmen are good communicators they will instinctively know how to use any material that improves their communication ability. The truth is that few men have a natural flair for using sales tools properly. Too many well-developed materials have ended up in the trunk of the car because the salesman "tried it a couple of times and it didn't do the job." The man in the field may believe that his customers will think he is being too aggressive or too stilted or too long-winded when he uses a selling aid to supplement his own personality. Unfortunately, the salesman is often correct—the material was poorly designed and not field tested. More often than not, however, the problem is in the training, in showing the man how to use the material properly and how to make it an extension of, rather than a substitute for, his own sales techniques.

Summary

Selling aids and programs are a tremendous lever for the sales manager, and he can sharply increase his sales force's success by providing imaginative assistance. He has already committed himself to the size and structure of his sales force and to his sales coverage plan. The quantity of sales effort he will get is fixed within narrow limits, but the quality is wide open for improvement.

The following checklist reviews all the steps that should be taken to develop selling tools. Completing it will help to focus attention on those areas where the greatest advances can be made. It may be a good idea to have the salesmen and supervisors fill out the same checklist, and see what they think of the material that has been provided. By bringing them into the discussion, it should be easier to agree on the future selling aids program and to insure that the men will do their best to use the material to make successful sales calls.

Checklist No. 11
Providing the Selling Tools

TOPIC	OK	NEEDS SOME WORK	KEY AREA FOR ATTEN-TION	DOES NOT APPLY
Defining the Types of Sales Calls				
1. The principal types of sales calls that our men make have been clearly defined.	____	____	____	____
2. Our salesmen have the material they need to make an effective presentation of our basic marketing program.	____	____	____	____
3. We periodically provide new selling aids that help our men make their regular planned coverage an interesting experience for our customers.	____	____	____	____
4. Every salesman has the tools he needs to move a prospect systematically through the steps of a purchase.	____	____	____	____
5. If our salesmen make training or service calls, they have the information and the technical aids needed to do a superior job.	____	____	____	____
6. Merchandising sales calls are successful because we supply all the materials and details to our men well in advance of the needed date.	____	____	____	____
7. Troubleshooting calls are handled positively, and our men have the knowl-				

Checklist No. 11
(Continued)

TOPIC	OK	NEEDS SOME WORK	KEY AREA FOR ATTEN- TION	DOES NOT APPLY
edge, authority, and equipment needed to make the customer feel he is being treated fairly.	⎯⎯	⎯⎯	⎯⎯	⎯⎯
8. Other important categories of sales calls have been studied, and the best selling tools we can devise have been provided.	⎯⎯	⎯⎯	⎯⎯	⎯⎯

Analysis of the Components of a Sales Call

We have carefully analyzed each of the major types of sales calls in terms of the eight basic parts of a call, and our men are well equipped for each component, including:

9. *Planning* They have correct and complete territory records and planning guides or checklists for the call.	⎯⎯	⎯⎯	⎯⎯	⎯⎯
10. *Approach* They have sales aids that help them make effective selling approaches to both present customers and prospects.	⎯⎯	⎯⎯	⎯⎯	⎯⎯
11. *Presentation* The most frequently used types of presentations are supported by pertinent and imaginative selling aids.	⎯⎯	⎯⎯	⎯⎯	⎯⎯
12. *Handling objections* The most common objections have been identified, and our salesmen have authoritative answers, backed by selling aids.	⎯⎯	⎯⎯	⎯⎯	⎯⎯

13. *Accomplishing the objective* The most important call objectives have been established, and powerful selling

Checklist No. 11
(Continued)

TOPIC	OK	NEEDS SOME WORK	KEY AREA FOR ATTEN-TION	DOES NOT APPLY
tools help our salesmen attain their specific call goals.	____	____	____	____
14. *Call-back foundation* We have developed materials and techniques that aid our salesmen in scheduling another call and in maintaining a strong selling position.	____	____	____	____
15. *Postcall analysis* Our men are encouraged to analyze their call results and to suggest changes in selling programs. We give them the authority and the funds to experiment with new ideas and tools.	____	____	____	____
16. *Recording* It is easy to complete the record of what happened on the call, and it can be done immediately.	____	____	____	____
17. No extra reports are required from the salesmen. Management gets its information from a copy of the salesman's record.	____	____	____	____

Identifying the Selling Aids and Sales Programs Needed

18. We have designed and given each salesman his basic selling equipment, including information about the company, its products, and its services; prices and terms; and efficient order-taking and recordkeeping materials.	____	____	____	____
19. Individual territory selling aids have been provided, and they are of the best quality, or else we have authorized each man to develop his own at our expense.	____	____	____	____

Checklist No. 11
(Continued)

TOPIC	OK	NEEDS SOME WORK	KEY AREA FOR ATTEN- TION	DOES NOT APPLY
20. Special selling aids have been created for each important market segment.	——	——	——	——
21. Salesmen can attain maximum in-person selling time because they have the best transportation and communication equipment we can provide.	——	——	——	——
22. We have developed coordinated sales campaigns, and provided our men with a planned method of achieving major selling targets.	——	——	——	——

Design and Field Testing

23. Our selling tools are designed to help our men reach clear, customer-oriented, realistic objectives.	——	——	——	——
24. We get help from experts in developing selling tools and use only top-quality artwork, materials, and production methods.	——	——	——	——
25. Every selling aid is field tested by both our best and weakest men. The results are given proper weight in the final design.	——	——	——	——
26. Selling tools are coordinated with the rest of the company merchandising program and reach our salesmen in advance of the need for them.	——	——	——	——

Instruction in Using Selling Aids and Sales Programs

27. All training in the use of sales tools is efficiently done. Our men are skilled in using our selling tools.	——	——	——	——

Checklist No. 11
(Continued)

TOPIC	OK	NEEDS SOME WORK	KEY AREA FOR ATTEN-TION	DOES NOT APPLY
28. The training program includes periodic reviews of sales tools to show how successful men use them and to remedy shortcomings.	——	——	——	——

Summary

29. We have a comprehensive assortment of selling aids and sales programs, and they help our salesmen make successful calls. No major voids exist.	——	——	——	——
30. Our supervisors and salesmen have also completed this checklist. They agree with the ratings I have given for items 1 through 29. We have also agreed on a program to provide even more effective selling tools.	——	——	——	——

12 / Leading, Appraising, and Improving

ALL managers must be leaders, and a sales manager must be a great leader. Other department heads often direct a close-knit group of people who operate machines, or work with figures, according to mathematical principles and standard procedures. The major leadership task is to promote efficient, harmonious accomplishment of repetitive tasks. The sales team, however, is scattered over a wide area, and opportunities for mutual support and encouragement are rare. Each territory is different, so each salesman needs a unique kind of stimulus, especially since he faces the active opposition of aggressive competitors.

Phase 5 in the development of a field sales program should begin with the sales manager turning the spotlight on himself and judging how well qualified he is for the leadership role he must fill.

The Sales Manager as a Leader

Because he automatically defines a task clearly before undertaking it, the sales manager's first action is to make sure that his own position guide is complete and up to date. What is he expected to accomplish, and what skills must he have to achieve outstanding performance? Just as he worked with each of his own salesmen in defining the job to be done, he should (and no doubt already has) turn to his own superior for counsel. The same type of position guide that is so effective for the sales force will work for him, and the two descriptions should blend into a single operating concept. His men must help him perform all his duties, and he must have the authority to aid them in reaching their objectives.

The next step is to rate himself and to determine what steps are to be taken to create or to improve the qualities he must possess. Humility has been defined as a just recognition of one's virtues and shortcomings; in effect, it is a candid appraisal. The attributes a sales manager should have can be divided into three categories: business, professional, and personal.

Business Skills

The definition of business skills includes how much he needs to know about his products, the markets he serves, and the company he represents. Is the required level of product knowledge so high that the sales manager must really be one of the best technicians in the company? There are businesses where in-depth knowledge is essential; it would be hard to visualize a good sales manager for a printing company who was not an expert in the craft. In other cases, knowledge of the market is the key factor, and the sales executive who thoroughly knows the grocery trade can move from product to product with relative ease.

Some sales managers will devise an effective training program for every person except themselves, perhaps because they cannot admit to being less than perfect in every phase of the business. The salesman in the field, however, will be more receptive to training when he sees that it extends to the entire supervisory and management group. Motivation by example is a powerful stimulant.

Professional Skills

The critical professional skills are knowledge of the science of sales management and knowledge of the art of leadership. By developing his own comprehensive field program, the sales manager has amply demonstrated that he knows his profession. He is a fully informed executive, thoroughly versed in the principles of his work, and completely competent to manage the selling operation. While sales management does require mastery of a body of knowledge, it also needs a warmth and a personal style that can best be described as artistic. The sales manager must be a very human leader, for sales forces should not be driven to success; far better if the men respond to a captain who is determined to show how good they are, not how good he is. The four main types of leadership needed in sales activity can be classified as emotional (subjective), intellectual (objective), short range (tactical), and long range (strategic). Proper blending of all four images will provide the salesmen the direction and stimulation they need to carry out the exciting plan that the sales manager has created.

Emotional or subjective leadership. A salesman spends most of his time dealing with people rather than things. He both creates and needs a warm relationship with his fellowman. Emotional leadership gives the individual and the group a feeling of comradeship without weakening the lines of authority. One general sales manager found that his best branch operation had a disastrous month at the height of the season. He flew out to see the branch manager, a long-time associate, who felt worse than anyone else. The afternoon was spent visiting a few key customers and telling them about the company's plans to launch a major new product. The evening hours were devoted to a long relaxing dinner. The boss left the following morning, never having visited the plant or the office, but having made it clear by his actions that he had absolute confidence in his best branch manager. This type of emotional leadership as practiced by a wise sales executive may have been at variance with the traditional approach to correcting deficiencies, but it was more effective than any "searching review."

Intellectual leadership. If the sales manager has gone through the process of completing his own position guide, analyzing his skills, and developing his personal training program, he will meet the test of intellectual leadership. The men in the field want a boss who understands the problem and who can help them find the best solution. Pat answers, pep talks, and glittering generalities fall on deaf ears. The need is for a sales manager who knows the business and knows it completely.

Short-range leadership. General George Patton was once termed the finest assault commander in Europe. It was a tribute to his short-range leadership skill. No great administrator, Patton could be counted on for massive help when things got tough. The all-around sales manager must create the same image. He must help his men attain their goals, and he must aid in problem solving, quickly and without undue criticism. If something in the field sales effort has gone off course, or fallen short of plan, management will do well to look first at itself when trying to fix the blame. The fault may not be in the performance, but in the basic plan. Perhaps the men were not given the tools they needed or not trained in their use. They may be overextended, frustrated, yet doing the best they can. Selling conditions in the field are always changing, and both problems and opportunities arise daily. The sales manager must be "an assault commander," standing up for his men and giving them immediate and forceful support when they need it.

Long-range leadership. The principal component of long-range leadership is the direct relationship with the sales team; it ties in closely with the motivation and career development phases of the sales program. A good salesman stays with the company because he believes his long-term objectives will be attained with his manager's help. In addition to his personal ambitions, each salesman wants the sales force to be a respected group, considered by all in the company as worthy members of the total market-oriented team.

The other aspect of long-range leadership involves the sales manager's relation with key executives. He must convince them that, as the company grows, he and his team will expand and improve in a systematic way. He must be seen as a long-range leader, not one trying to build personal success by climbing over the prostrate bodies of his associates and then leaving for greener pastures.

Personal Attributes

If there is one personal quality a sales manager must possess it is unflagging optimism. He must be convinced, and be able to convince others, that the outcome will always be the best possible under the circumstances. There's no need to be a Pollyanna, naively saying, "Every day in every way things are getting better and better." Being an unflagging optimist means believing that the most advantageous solution can and will be found. Field selling is synonymous with confrontation; actions and reactions occur constantly, and problems arise. A sales manager must be realistic, but only if he first and always is optimistic. If by nature he looks for the worst case, or the disadvantages of a proposal, then he shouldn't be the sales manager. The field salesmen want a man who will help them achieve success, not one who is dedicated to saving them from failure.

Other necessary personal attributes are related to the nature of the business and to the sales manager's position guide. The ability to speak to large groups is a common requirement. So is a knowledge of the techniques of high-level, complicated negotiation. Perhaps the mission of the field salesman is to bring the account to the comparison stage and have his superior take over for the final give-and-take necessary to bring conviction and action. Facility in more than one language and excellence or at least adequacy in a sport or form of recreation are other examples of the individual abilities that a sales manager may need. Identifying and cataloging these abilities make it easier for the sales manager to attain the necessary skill level and to secure company support and funds for the schooling or experience required. When he has completed his self-examination and judged his own leadership qualities, the sales manager can turn to a consideration of how to use those skills to direct his team.

The Meaning of Management Control

Management is defined as the direction of an operation. The role of the manager is to take charge of a unit and to guide it to the attainment of its objectives. Most of this book has been devoted to the first three steps of the management cycle: planning, organizing, and delegating. As he gets his organization into operation, the manager increasingly practices the other major management functions: leading, appraising, and changing. Leadership is synonymous with direction; the several kinds of leadership that are essential have just been discussed.

In exercising management control over salesmen, the leader must be especially careful to be seen as a participant, and not as an outsider. One business school lecturer was fond of saying that the last cry that would come from misguided management would probably be, "If I told them once, I told them a hundred times." No sales manager can take such an attitude; it must be "we," "our program," "our customers," and especially "our (not the) production department."

Appraisal. The best appraisal system is based on the company's existing management information system, not on parallel records kept by the sales department. Throughout this book, the need for one set of data has been heavily stressed, and it is assumed that the field sales program is completely integrated into the company-wide gathering of facts and figures. When it comes to the appraisal of the stream of information, the correct attitude is an extension of the leadership philosophy that must permeate sales management. The atmosphere that should be created is one of an organized search for improvement, and not a hunt for deficiencies. By emphasizing the positive side it is possible to win the support of all in the attempt to do things better. Looking for shortcomings inevitably splits people into two groups, prosecutors and defendants, and that is not the way to run a sales force. The Greeks have a saying, "There are no failures; there are only degrees of success."

The concept of management by exception has been popular as a means of focusing attention on those factors that most need scrutiny. The theory is good, but too often the practice can better be described as management by (exception), in which the initial approach is to hunt among the figures for the parentheses that indicate performance below plan. This can be a sound approach when the operation is based on a rated capacity, as with a chemicals plant or a production line. Sales management, however, consists just as much of exploiting opportunities as it does of remedying any shortcomings. The appraisal system, by whatever name called, must illuminate the growth areas as well as the problems.

Making improvements by making changes. The final step in the management cycle, the appraisal, leads smoothly into the first step of a new management cycle, for a decision to change a plan automatically raises the question, "What is the new plan?" A sales manager will rarely find that he has all the facts that should be at his command when the time for decision draws near. Competitors do not mail him advance copies of their field selling plans, and he can only hope that it means they do not have a formal plan. When pricing problems arise, it is hard to separate fact from rumor, claim from bluff, or to measure the consequences of the pricing decision that must be made. And yet, he has pledged himself to be a leader, to act decisively.

Regulating the time for analysis so that it is appropriate to the dimensions of the decision is one rule for dynamic sales management. If a judgment must be made about meeting a competitive price on one sale to one customer, speedy action is needed and usually relatively easy to take. On the other hand, a break in price with a major account will probably require the extension of that price to all similar customers, and will often trigger price reactions from competitors. As he appraises his entire program, the sales manager must continually ask himself two questions, "How can this be improved?" and "What are the dimensions of the change I am contemplating?" If he acts rapidly when the facts permit, and prudently when large sales issues are at stake, he will maintain his correct leadership balance and earn the continued support of his men in the field.

A Sales Manager's Major Control Areas

The key areas of sales management control fall into three categories: local program development, unit and individual performance, and relations with others. If leadership is, in large part, setting a good example, a fine start has been made toward effective direction of the first category, local program development. Because he has built his own comprehensive plan, the sales manager can logically require each supervisor and territory manager to create a similar one covering the same components of the selling task.

Developing Local Programs

Each sales unit, whether territory, branch, or region, is a management unit, and the man in charge must think and act like a manager. He has six major goals:

- To organize his area, his customers, and his prospects into an efficient selling unit that can be worked in a planned sequence.
- To increase the business done with present customers.
- To add new customers and to expand into new markets.
- To improve the profitability of his operation.
- To increase the efficiency with which he operates, and to help his customers and his company associates work more efficiently.
- To administer his operation in a superior way, so that the company's business is properly handled and correctly accounted for.

The preparation of the local sales program is divided into three steps. Initially, the field force must tell the manager what can be accomplished during the coming year, and what tools and funds will be needed. As the sales manager assembles these field forecasts, he has the opportunity to compare them with the plan that the company executives are beginning to develop.

The second stage is mutual agreement on the goals. Having made their preliminary forecast, the field units now receive in return the company's ideas on the goals that should be set, and the major programs that should be launched or continued. In a candid and helpful way, the central office and the local units thrash out areas of disagreement, and an approved standard of performance is established.

The final step is the preparation of the specific program for attaining the required performance. Key account campaigns must be organized and sales coverage plans brought up to date. The field units must set up their own schedules that will mesh with the company's merchandising and product introduction programs. In Chapter 1 the three principal benefits of a company profit plan were defined as commitment, freedom, and concentration; territory and unit sales programs bring the same benefits. The man in the field is *committed* to a level of achievement, and his sales manager is committed to giving him full support. The unit or territory manager has risen far above the ranks of the ordinary salesman or supervisor, because he now has great *freedom* of action within the framework of his plan. And, finally, the market-oriented philosophy has triumphed again, as everyone from the president to the newest salesman *concentrates* on the same objectives.

Unit and Individual Performance

A full package of motivating forces — compensation, incentives and contests, and career development — has been created to help the sales manager get the ultimate in selling effort from his men. He is a participating leader who is constantly with his field force — counseling, recognizing achievement, making changes. His periodic reviews are mutual searches for improvement, not "hell sessions" in which the manager criticizes and the salesman sulks. Much of the success of this program of appraisal and change is due to the careful way that he established yardsticks to measure progress in every important aspect of field selling.

Rating unit performance

Performance against plan. The key indicators of results were set when the sales volume, selling profit, and selling expense tasks were defined. The sales information system should be organized so that the regular reports of selling activity include figures to show variance from plan. Management by exception (with equal emphasis on gains and losses) points out the areas that need change.

Account coverage. A very good advance indicator of what sales will be like in the future can be obtained by studying present sales activity. Overconcentration on existing and small accounts will mean too few new buyers and will surely endanger the company's position with its key customers. Salesmen can fall into travel patterns, sometimes not realizing how often they call on certain accounts and how badly they are neglecting remote or highly competitive areas. The appraisal program must therefore include some uncomplicated way of comparing actual calling patterns with the guidelines that the sales manager has set up.

Successful sales calls. Sales activity is one measure of performance, but sales success must also be determined. Each salesman has been equipped with the best sales aids and selling programs the company can devise, but do they work? Are the salesmen using them, and is there a steady stream of orders that documents the effectiveness of the many calls being made?

Key customer campaigns. The sales manager cannot keep track of progress with each account, but he should certainly know every key customer personally and have at his fingertips a status report that shows the progress made with these major buyers. Each one has been worthy of a separate sales campaign and thus is also worthy of individual appraisal.

Training programs. Periodic appraisal of the training needs has produced a continuing training program, composed of both group and individual activity. A sales manager must be on guard against letting the pressure for immediate orders cause the postponement of training. If the need to develop skills has been defined, the education process must proceed, despite the ups and downs of sales volume, with proper timing and with provision for major crises. Sales meetings are not held during the height of the season, and a critical inventory problem may dictate that selling, and selling alone, must be the rule for a brief interval.

Size and structure of the sales force. As the sales campaign unfolds, the decisions about the size and structure of the sales force must be reexamined. Has the company been able to recruit the type of men it needs, and are they proving to be the right salesmen for the market segments they serve? Are the men underemployed with too few accounts, or are they overextended and unable to service customers and prospects as planned? Is the distribution system proving to be effective? Should there be more or fewer supervisors?

Morale. If the sales force sees the right people and makes effective calls, it should produce the planned sales results. Unit and individual accomplishments should be publicized and rewarded, but sometimes the pressure of sales problems distracts management from recognizing the sales successes. What is the attitude of the men in the field? Are they "up," or have they lost that inner spark?

Other tasks. Clear assignments have been given to the sales force, and there are specific nonselling tasks that must be performed on time and correctly. Open communication with other departments is usually the best method of appraising field performance of these extra duties. The accounting manager will have very definite ideas about how well the sales administration functions are being done, but the sales manager must listen and learn and not go on the offensive when constructive criticism is leveled.

Recordkeeping. There are no standard solutions that will fit exactly an individual company's need to keep track of all the above components of the field sales task. Some systems for listing calls and sales results and for maintaining territory records have been devised by companies specializing in recordkeeping; they are worth investigation. Having developed a field sales program that is worthy of his growing company, the sales manager must be sure that he has also set up the monitoring and control system he needs. Earlier in the book, it was said that the question "How's business?" triggered the immediate response "Compared to what?" The second question has been answered by the establishment of goals and standards of performance, and now the first question needs answering.

Rating individual performance

No program for appraisal and change is complete unless it includes a measurement of the performance of each man on the sales force. Many companies have experimented with systems for ranking the accomplishments of each individual, but often the result is too complicated or too controversial. One good solution is to separate the sales force into three groups: the best performers, the weakest performers, and those whose results fall into the "good to fair" ranking. One company with about 100 salesmen felt that it really could not say which salesman was the best and which one was the worst. It did, however, devise a system that identified the top 10 percent and the bottom 10 percent. The best men were obviously those who had to be retained either through promotion or a program of parallel development. The weakest performers required prompt training or separation.

The sales manager selected four categories of sales activity, and within each one ranked all his men according to the results attained. For example, performance against quota was one measurement, and the man with the highest percentage of accomplishment was ranked No. 1. Another factor in the rating was the percentage of total sales represented by a high-margin group of products. Ability to add new customers to the books and the amount of accounts receivable in relation to total sales were other indicators. Each man's ranking in all four categories was totaled, and the man with the lowest cumulative amount became No. 1 in the overall ranking. He was never told so, because the procedure did not pretend to give exact standings; it could only identify those whose performance across the board was excellent and those who were substandard. The final list is like the accompanying chart, grouping the best and weakest men:

Salesman	Quota Rank	Premium Products Rank	New Account Rank	Receivables Rank	Total	Overall Rank
The Top 10%						
Brown, Arthur	1	21	8	3	33	1
Carter, James	19	4	11	7	41	2
Crowell, Henry	4	7	9	23	43	3
Allan, B. T.	6	18	2	19	45	4
Maxwell, Robert	3	16	14	17	50	5
The Bottom 10%						
Rogers, Samuel	63	56	93	43	255	99
Amberg, Joseph	91	79	81	33	284	100
Weber, C. M.	76	83	98	58	315	101
Farrell, William	84	81	86	93	344	102
McLean, Donald	100	94	87	77	358	103

The results of the rating were never published, but they did form the basis for action on management's part. The best men were given special assignments and recognition, and every effort was made to keep them happy and productive. They and their work were studied to see what made them such good salesmen and what lessons could be learned that would improve the selection and training programs for new men. The low men received individual counseling, and their general standard of performance was discussed with them frankly. Extra training saved some of them, but in many cases it was clear to both parties that the salesman would be more productive in another job or with another company.

Relations with Others

Although most of his management duties involve his own team, the sales manager also works with other departments in the company, as well as with people outside the organization whose support is essential. In this external leadership he has an opportunity to build the reputation of his own men, and through them, to win credit for himself.

The company-wide search for improvement

In the market-oriented company the improvement process is continuous. Every day there is a search for a better way to serve the customer, and at intervals there is a major appraisal of the basic goals and strategies. The field sales manager is a key participant, since he is usually in closer touch with the demand market segments than any other company executive, and he must interpret the customer's needs. His role is not to provide answers so much as it is to raise questions, to point out opportunities, and to predict future patterns of demand.

Feedback systems. One test of a sales manager's external leadership is the kind of feedback system he has organized to report what is happening in the marketplace. The defensive manager emphasizes defensive reporting; prices are weak, competition has gone crazy, and the quality and performance of what he sells cause him constant problems. Such a sales manager finds that he carries no weight in the company's debating of alternatives; he is a pessimistic critic and is treated as such.

His aim should be to design a system that accurately reports what customers and prospects think, what the acceptance of new products is likely to be, and what competitive moves can be expected. It must filter and transmit, and not be a system that is collapsing under its own weight, producing reams of reports that are never read. The starting point can often be a searching discussion with other company executives, determining what they want to know and what kind of documentation is needed for the reports that will be made. A good checkpoint along the way is to discontinue all feedback reports without notice and wait to see who screams. One sales manager cut out a certain periodic report, heard nothing for seven months, and ultimately found out that the report was originated by a man since retired; no one else read it.

Getting along with others

Customer advisory panels. Excellent intelligence can be obtained from customers if they are given an appropriate opportunity to express themselves. Some of the rules for successful customer advisory panels include:

- Absolutely without fail, all company executives who are due to attend conferences with customers must attend. No more direct slight can be devised than to bring important people together and have them find out that they are meeting the "second team."

- Don't argue. The company asked for the customer's opinion; accept it. Expression of another opinion by the company may be acceptable, but efforts to change people's positions during group meetings should be avoided.

- Emphasize common interests. The customers must be able to identify with each other. Wholesalers won't talk discounts in front of consumers, and presidents won't express their candid views in front of assistant department managers.

The image inside the company. One sure way to damage the process of appraisal and improvement is to create the feeling that market oriented means marketing dominated. True, the sales manager must see that his men get just recognition and that they have a fair share of the company's resources. He is the man who built the sales force, but his central dedication is the same as that of every other employee—to serve the customer. Because field sales results are so visible they sometimes invite criticism without justification, or they can be overemphasized, to the resentment of other departments. A tolerant, cooperative attitude is needed; let others have their say, so long as there is only one dominant factor— the customer.

The image outside the company. An effective sales manager will have built a strong personal relationship with his key customers and prospects. He may already be doing a good job of balancing his contributions to industry activity against the danger of being called on for too much help. No one needs to tell him that criticizing his company or any part of it will hurt his standing in the eyes of those on the outside. A good sales manager brings out a positive response from customers, friends, and competitors. And each man must ask himself how he qualifies in this regard, as well as in all the other aspects of leading, appraising, and improving as listed in the following, and final, checklist.

The Complete, but Forever Incomplete, Field Sales Program

A field sales program developed in accordance with the plan outlined in this book *must* be successful. Every major aspect of sales management has been analyzed and the alternatives studied. Each component of the program has been fitted with all the others so that they make a single unit. The titles and numbers on the manning table have been transformed into a dynamic team of highly skilled specialists, and they are well trained, powerfully motivated, and superbly equipped. It looks as though the task is complete, but of course it never is.

After completing the following checklist, it might be a good idea to turn back to Chapter 2, in which all the program components were summarized, and to reflect again on "Where do we go from here?" Whatever the answer, the sales manager in the market-oriented company is indeed a fortunate man. He accomplishes his tasks in an atmosphere that makes his work not a job, but an opportunity. He can help himself, he can help his associates, but most of all he can help his customers.

Checklist No. 12
Leading, Appraising, and Improving

TOPIC	OK	NEEDS SOME WORK	KEY AREA FOR ATTEN- TION	DOES NOT APPLY

The Sales Manager as a Leader

1. I have a position guide that is complete and up to date. It has been developed jointly with my superior and he agrees that it defines my responsibilities and the results expected from me.

2. The business skills that I need have been enumerated, including the level of knowledge required about my company, our products, and our markets. An individual training program is in effect to improve those skills.

3. The professional skills I should have in the field of sales management have also been defined and a program established to impart or improve each skill.

4. I have analyzed the four types of leadership and have decided what my sales force needs from me. I am providing the right kind of leadership.

5. Other personal attributes I should possess have been identified, and I have a planned method of developing or improving those qualities.

Exercising Management Control

6. An efficient data system gives me prompt and accurate reports of major sales force activities.

7. Our method of appraising sales force performance is a positive one and emphasizes growth opportunities as much as the remedying of deficiencies.

Checklist No. 12
(Continued)

TOPIC	OK	NEEDS SOME WORK	KEY AREA FOR ATTEN- TION	DOES NOT APPLY
8. We regulate the amount of study that precedes a change by the dimensions of the decision. We act both promptly *and* prudently.	——	——	——	——
A Sales Manager's Major Control Areas				
9. Each sales unit and sales territory is required to make an annual plan that is realistic and attainable.	——	——	——	——
10. We regularly appraise unit and in-dividual performance against our plan for each of our major sales objectives.	——	——	——	——
11. We record enough data about our salesmen's calls to confirm that the sales coverage guidelines I have estab-lished are in fact being followed in the field.	——	——	——	——
12. Call results are analyzed, and we know if our men are making successful calls and if the selling aids and sales programs are doing their job.	——	——	——	——
13. We have direct and personal knowl-edge of the success of individual cam-paigns directed at key customers and prospects.	——	——	——	——
14. Our training program is monitored, and we know if it is on schedule and if it is attaining its objectives.	——	——	——	——
15. The structure, size, and location of our sales force are periodically ex-amined, and sound changes are made.	——	——	——	——
16. The morale of our sales force is high. We recognize achievements and reward accomplishments.	——	——	——	——

Checklist No. 12
(Continued)

TOPIC	OK	NEEDS SOME WORK	KEY AREA FOR ATTEN- TION	DOES NOT APPLY
17. I know how well we are performing our other duties, including our nonselling tasks. I regularly seek the counsel of other interested department heads.	_____	_____	_____	_____
18. Looking at our overall recordkeeping system, I would rate it as efficient. It is not too voluminous or burdensome, and it provides prompt and accurate data to all sales force members.	_____	_____	_____	_____
19. We have developed ways to measure the comparative performance of individual salesmen. We periodically rank our salesmen, identifying the strongest and weakest performers.	_____	_____	_____	_____
20. We make sure that our best men receive special training, proper compensation, and assistance in career development.	_____	_____	_____	_____
21. Our weakest performers are either trained to an acceptable level of performance or are separated or have been reassigned. We do not retain substandard salesmen.	_____	_____	_____	_____

"External" Leadership

TOPIC	OK	NEEDS SOME WORK	KEY AREA FOR ATTEN- TION	DOES NOT APPLY
22. I participate effectively in the company-wide search for improvements, and others welcome my efforts.	_____	_____	_____	_____
23. We have developed an efficient feedback system to tell us what customers and prospects are thinking and what environmental changes are occurring in the marketplace.	_____	_____	_____	_____

Checklist No. 12
(Continued)

TOPIC	OK	NEEDS SOME WORK	KEY AREA FOR ATTEN-TION	DOES NOT APPLY
24. The field sales group gets along well with other departments. We are respected contributors to the company's success.	____	____	____	____
25. I enjoy excellent relations with customers, influence groups or persons, and industry associates.	____	____	____	____

Index